Contents

First printing June, 1996

Published by Quilt in a Day®, Inc.
1955 Diamond St.
San Marcos, CA 92069

1996© Eleanor A. Burns Family Trust

ISBN 0-922705-89-5

Editor Loretta Smith
Assistant Editor Robin Green
Art Director Merritt Voigtlander
Assistant Art Director Susan Sells

Yardage

Fabric for Twelve Star Blocks *

12" Finished Size

The cover quilt features Benartex Fabrics. The "zinger," a large-scale paisley print in multiple tones of turkey red, indigo blue, and beige, pulls the quilt together. The various textures in the prints add excitement to the quilt.

BENARTEX
INCORPORATED

First Color Family

1 yd first dark

¾ yd first medium

¼ yd first light medium

Begin by selecting a multi-colored fabric as a large-scale floral with three or four colors in a dark value. This should be the "zinger," or the most attractive piece in your quilt. From that multi-colored fabric, select two color families that complement each other. Of those two colors, select different values as dark, medium, and light medium. The "zinger" can be one of the dark values. Values are interchangeable in the blocks as long as there is the desired contrast. Vary the textures of the prints, as large scale, medium scale and small scale. Include several that read solid from a distance.

Follow these yardage guidelines, or be creative and plan your own choices of values and number of fabrics to total the same.

Second Color Family

1 yd second dark

¾ yd second medium

¼ yd second light medium

Background

1½ yds of one light
    four 3½" wide strips into…
       …48 – 3½" squares

one 7½" wide strip into…
      …five 7½" squares

one 7¼" wide strip into…
      …five 7¼" squares

Choose a light value fabric for background which appears solid from a distance, or a non-distracting small print. It must be light enough to contrast with the other fabric. Good choices are muslin, white print on muslin, or white print on white fabric.

Use these pieces as they are called for in blocks. Refer to each block for additional background pieces.

---

* The blank square to the left is provided for you to paste in your own fabric swatches.

Fabric for Twelve Block Setting of Your Choice

Your Choices Include...

Four Point Star Setting
See page 105.

Size before borders 56" x 71"

Eight Point Star Setting
See page 108.

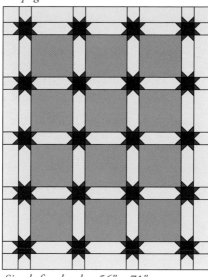

Size before borders 56" x 71"

Kaleidoscope Star Setting
See page 110.

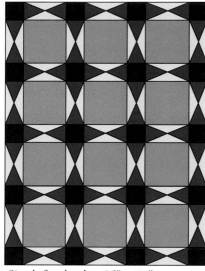

Size before borders 56" x 73"

Fabric for All Choices

Background
2¼ yds

Star Points
1⅛ yds

Star Centers
½ yd

Fabric for Additional Borders *Cut strips selvage to selvage.*

First Border
¾ yd

eight 3" wide strips
Approximate Size 61" x 76"

Second Border
1¾ yds

nine 6" wide strips
Approximate Size 72" x 87"

Third Border
3 yds

eleven 9" wide strips
Approximate Size 89" x 104"

Binding
1 yd

eleven 3" wide strips

Backing
Purchase after top is finished.

Bonded Batting
Purchase after top is finished.

Techniques

Cutting Instructions

Instead of providing template shapes to construct the blocks, measurements are given. Use a large size rotary cutter with a sharp blade on a gridded cutting mat. Different sizes of plexiglass rulers are available to make cutting easier.

Color Codes

The yardage chart on page two is color coded for the cover quilt. Instructions for each block are coded for a first color family (the blues) and a second color family (the reds). If you desire, paste small pieces of your fabric on page two and follow the code.

This is an example from the first block, on page 10. Each patch is color coded to indicate which fabrics to cut and use in the step-by-step directions.

 one 4" x 8" rectangle first medium
one 4" x 8" rectangle first dark

Cutting Pieces

Following the example, select first medium and first dark. Press right sides together with the lighter of the two on top, lining up selvage edges on a corner of the fabric.

Place the 12½" Square Up ruler on the layered fabric with the 1" measurement in the upper right corner. Layer cut the pieces slightly larger than 4" x 8".

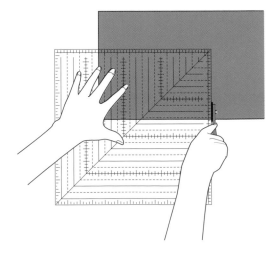

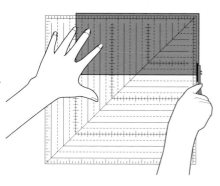

Turn the pieces, and cut to the exact size of 4" x 8". Pieces cut right sides together are now ready for sewing instructions on the second page of each block.

Use the 12½" Square Up ruler for cutting any squares or rectangles less than 12½". Solo pieces are cut in single layers.

Cutting Squares

Use the 6" square ruler for cutting pieces smaller than 6". For several squares the same size, cut a strip that measurement first, and then cut the squares.

Cutting on the Diagonal

Line up the 45º line on a 6" x 12" or 6" x 24" ruler with the left edge of the square and cut.

Some patches are cut on both diagonals. Keep square intact until both cuts are made.

"Fussy Cuts"

To do "fussy cuts," center the design within the designated size square. Cut on two sides. Turn, center the design within the square, and cut on the remaining two sides.

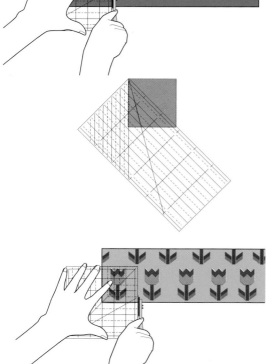

Fold

Cutting Strips

When cutting rectangles and squares, cut from one raw edge of the fabric.

Cut strips **selvage to selvage** from the opposite side of the fabric with 6" x 12" or 6" x 24" ruler. Straighten the raw edge. Move your ruler over until the ruler lines are at the newly cut edge. Carefully and accurately line up and cut the strips at the measurements given.

Thread

Use a neutral colored thread. An off-white, gray or light blue thread usually blends with any colors. If you are using a bright white fabric, use white thread.

Stitches per Inch

Use 15 stitches per inch, or 2 to 2.5 on machines with stitch selections from 1 to 4.

Assembly-line Sewing

Save time and thread when sewing several paired pieces by butting one after another without cutting the thread or removing from the machine.

Use the stiletto to help push patches under the presser foot and hold your seams flat as you sew over them.

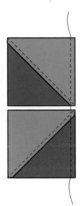

The Grid Method

Patches of two triangles start with two fabrics layered, pressed right sides together, and cut as a square or rectangle.

Draw a grid of squares as specified on the wrong side of the layered fabric. Use the lines of the cutting mat to line up the ruler.

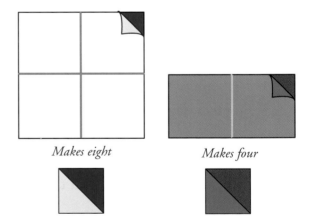

Makes eight   *Makes four*

Marking

With a pencil, draw diagonal lines across the grid so you can continuously sew ¼" on both sides of the line. Pin.

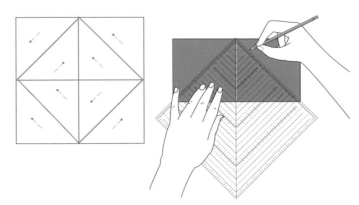

Sewing

Sew an accurate and consistent ¼" seam allowance. Sew a few stitches ¼" from the diagonal line. Check by measuring between the line and the stitching. If necessary, make adjustments by changing your needle position, or your foot until your seam is ¼".

Press the sewn grid to set the seam. Cut on the horizontal and vertical lines, then cut on the diagonals.

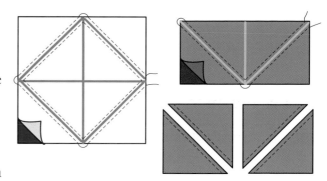

Pressing

Lay the pieces on the ironing board with the darker fabric on top. Open the triangles, pressing the seam allowance to the darker fabric, unless you are directed to press to the lighter fabric for easier construction. Press carefully to avoid leaving folds at seam lines. Using steam is a personal preference.

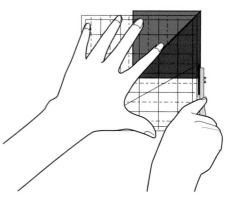

Squaring Up Oversized Blocks

Squaring Up with a Square Ruler

Trim the oversized patch to the specified size using the 6" Square Up ruler or 12½" Square Up ruler. Lay the ruler's diagonal line on the seam, and trim two edges.

Turn the patch and lay the diagonal line on the seam. Place the ruler lines of the specified measurement on the newly cut edges, and trim the final edges.

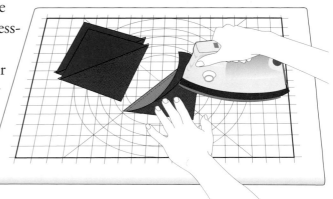

Squaring Up with a Rectangular Ruler

Use a Quilt in a Day® 6" x 12" ruler with dashed diagonal lines at 45°.

The example is for a 4½" square. Before the square is pressed open, position the ruler's 4½" dashed line on the upper edge of the stitching. Center ruler along stitching. Cut on both edges of the ruler. Trim tips. Press open.

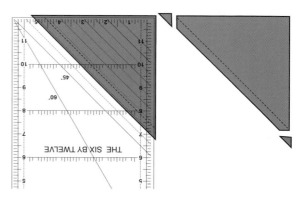

The Flying Geese Method

This technique is used in five blocks and several border treatments. The example is a 7½" Background square centered on a 9" Dark square to produce four 3½" x 6½" Flying Geese patches.

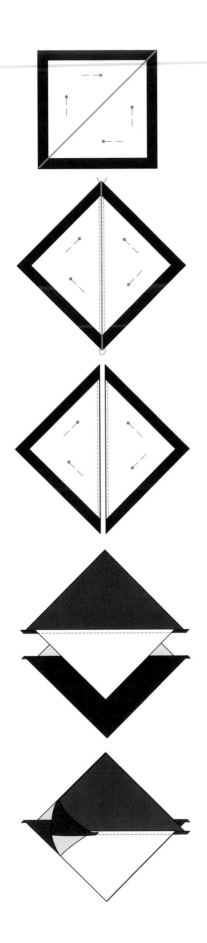

1. Place the smaller square right sides together and centered on the larger square. Press.

2. With the 6" x 24" ruler, draw a diagonal line across the squares. Pin.

3. Sew exactly ¼" from both sides of drawn line. Press to set seam.

4. Cut on drawn line. Press seam allowance to larger triangle.

5. Place squares right sides together so that opposite fabrics touch.

6. **Match up the outside edges.** Notice that there is a gap between the seams. The seams **do not lock.**

7. Draw a diagonal line across the seams. Pin.

8. Sew ¼" from both sides of drawn line. Press to set seam.

9. Cut on the drawn line.

10. Clip the seam allowance to the vertical seam midway between the horizontal seams. This allows the seam allowance to be pressed to the fabric of the original larger square.

11. Press each half open, pushing the clipped seam allowance to the fabric of the larger square.

12. With a 6" x 24" ruler or 6" x 12" ruler, line up the 45º line on a Geese seam, and the ¼" line on the peak. *The Quilt in a Day® 6" x 12" ruler is ideal for this step.*

13. Cut across, keeping **an exact** ¼" seam allowance beyond each peak.

14. Turn second piece and repeat. A small strip will be cut out of center.

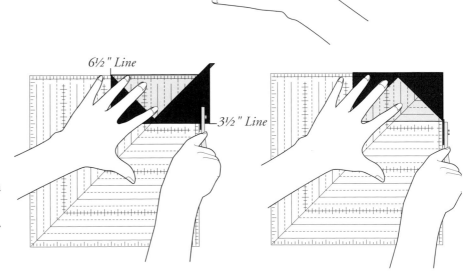

This example produces four patches 3½" x 6½".

15. With the 12½" ruler, place the diagonal line on the seam. Line up the bottom edge of the patch with the 3½" line on the ruler. Line up the left edge at 6½". Trim right and top edge. Turn and trim right edge to a perfect 3½" x 6½".

This technique produces four Flying Geese patches. The seam allowance is apparent only at the peak. Make sure the seams end in the corners.

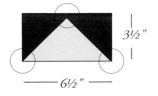

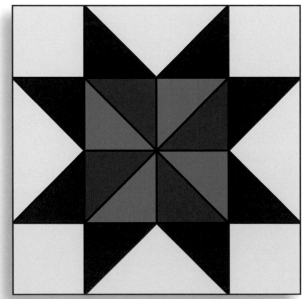

Barbara Frietchie Star

Barbara Frietchie was ninety-five when Confederate troops occupied her hometown of Frederick, Maryland. Unlike most citizens of Frederick, she did not try to conceal her Union sympathies. When the Southern troops began to leave the city, they passed directly by her house, where Barbara stood waving a Union flag. Despite threats and persuasions, she would not yield her flag to the Confederates. Finally, an officer gave the order that Barbara be permitted to wave her flag as long as she pleased. This quilt pattern has long been dedicated to Barbara Frietchie for her courage and patriotism.

Cutting Instructions

Layer cut right sides together:

 one 4" x 8" rectangle first medium
one 4" x 8" rectangle first dark

Cut:

 one 7½" square background
one 9" square second dark

 four 3½" squares background

Suggested values: choose the background, two darks, and one medium.

Making the Center

See Grid Method, page 6.

1. Use the 4" x 8" rectangles. Draw a 4" grid of two squares.

2. Draw on diagonal lines.

3. Sew ¼" from diagonal lines. Cut apart.

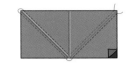

4. Drop on pressing mat with dark on top. Press to set seam. Open and press. Seam is behind darker fabric.

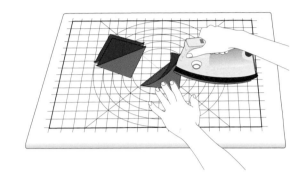

5. Square four patches to 3½".

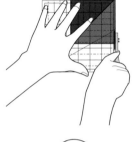

6. Lay out the four center patches.

7. Flip the right patches to the left, matching the outside edges. Assembly-line sew the vertical seam.

8. Sew the horizontal seam pushing the seam allowances in opposite directions and locking the seams.

9. Press. Patchwork should measure 6½" square. If not, check your original pieces and seams, and make an adjustment.

Making Four Flying Geese Patches

1. Right sides together, center the 7½" square on the 9" square.

2. Sew, following Flying Geese method on page 8.

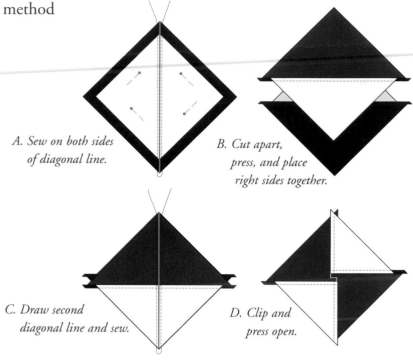

A. Sew on both sides of diagonal line.

B. Cut apart, press, and place right sides together.

C. Draw second diagonal line and sew.

D. Clip and press open.

3. Trim out four 3½" x 6½" Flying Geese patches.

Sewing the Block Together

1. Lay out the center square, corner squares, and Flying Geese patches.

2. Flip the middle row to the left. Match and pin the Flying Geese peak with the seam of the center square. Assembly-line sew the vertical seam.

3. Open and add the right row.

4. Sew the horizontal seams pushing the seams in opposite and consistent directions.

How to press seams is personal preference. The block lies flat when seams are pressed away from Geese. However, seams may show behind background corners from right side. For that reason, you may choose to press seams toward Geese.

5. Press. Measure your block. It should measure 12½" square. If it varies ⅛", blocks can be eased or stretched to fit together in quilt.

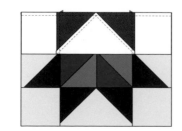

Border Treatment by Karen Strausheim

Yardage for Five Blocks

 Background . . . . . ½ yd

 First dark . . . . . ¼ yd

 Second dark . . . . ⅝ yd

 First medium . . . ¼ yd

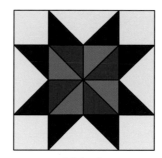

Make five

Additional Yardage for Quilt

Background . . . . 3 yds

 Solid blocks
        four 12½" squares
                (or size of your patchwork block)
Borders
        ten 3½" wide strips
Pieced border
        two 9" wide strips…
                …seven 9" squares
        two 7½" wide strips…
                …seven 7½" squares
        one 6½" wide strip…
               … four 6½" squares

Second dark . . . . . . 1¼ yds

 Pieced border
        two 9" wide strips…
                …seven 9" squares
        two 7½" wide strips…
                …seven 7½" squares
        four 3½" squares

Binding . . . . ⅝ yd

         six 3" wide strips

54" x 54"

Backing . . . . 3¼ yds

Batting . . . . 58" square

Sewing the Quilt Top Together

1. Lay out the star blocks and solid blocks.

2. Sew the vertical seams.

3. Sew the horizontal seams.

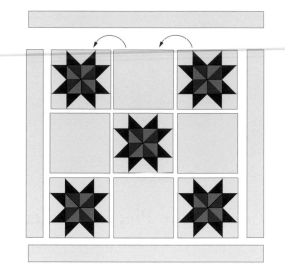

Adding the Inner Border

1. Add 3½" border strips to sides.

2. Add top and bottom border strips.

Making the Pieced Border

See Flying Geese Method, page 8.

1. Use the 9" and 7½" squares to make (28) 3½" x 6½" Flying Geese patches.

2. Make 28 Flying Geese, reversing the fabrics.

3. Sew pairs together to form the point. They should measure 6½" square.

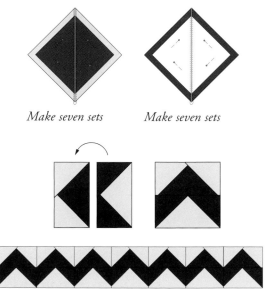

Make seven sets   *Make seven sets*

4. Sew seven pairs together for each border.

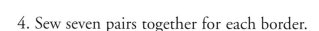

Making Border Corners for the Top and Bottom Strips

1. Draw a diagonal line on the back of four 3½" pieced border squares.

2. Lay a 3½" square right sides to a corner of each 6½" background square.

3. Sew **on the diagonal line** and trim ¼" from seam.

4. Press open. They should measure 6½" square.

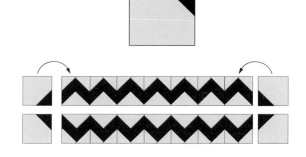

5. Sew a corner block to each end of two pieced borders for the top and bottom.

Adding the Pieced Border

1. Sew two pieced borders to the sides of the quilt.

If necessary, trim the inner borders to fit the pieced border.

2. Sew the two pieced borders with corner blocks to the top and bottom.

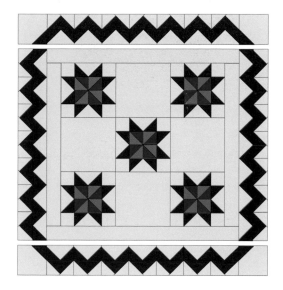

Adding the Outer Border

1. Add 3½" outer border strips to sides.

2. Add top and bottom border strips.

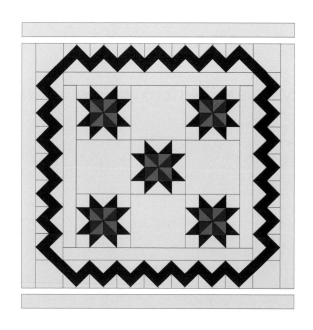

Harriet Tubman Star

Called "Moses" because she led her people to freedom, Harriet Tubman was a leader of the underground railroad. She made nineteen journeys out of the South, leading slaves to Northern states. When the Civil War began, Harriet joined Union forces as an unpaid nurse on the front lines. She also worked as a spy, going to Southern farms and plantations, where she gathered information from slaves. In her travels, she convinced slaves that the North was sincere in its promise of freedom. Many were inspired to join the Union army after hearing her speak. Because of her extensive knowledge of the land, she was a valuable scout and led several Union raids in Southern territory. After the war, Harriet moved to Auburn, New York, where she opened a home for elderly blacks.

Cutting Instructions

Cut:

 one 7½" square background
one 9" square first dark

 one 4½" square first light medium
one 6" square second dark

 four 2" squares first light medium

 one 3½" square second medium or "fussy cut"

 four 3½" squares background

Suggested values: choose the background, two darks, a medium, and a light medium.

Making Four Flying Geese Patches

1. Right sides together, center the 7½" square on the 9" square.

2. Sew, following Flying Geese method, page 8.

3. Trim out four 3½" x 6½" Flying Geese patches.

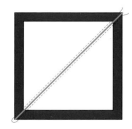

3½" x 6½"

Making Four Small Flying Geese Patches

1. Repeat with 4½" and 6" squares.

2. Trim out four 2" x 3½" Flying Geese patches.

2" x 3½"

Sewing the Block Together

1. Lay out the 3½" center square, four 2" squares, and small Flying Geese patches.

2. Flip the middle row to the left, and assembly-line sew the vertical seam.

3. Open and add the right row.

4. Sew the horizontal seams, pushing the scams in opposite directions, away from the Geese.

5. Press horizontal seams toward the center. The block should measure 6½".

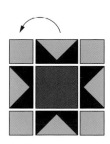

6. Lay out the center star, corner squares, and Flying Geese patches.

7. Flip the middle row to the left, and assembly-line sew the vertical seam.

8. Open and add the right row.

9. Sew the horizontal seams, pushing the seams in opposite directions toward the Geese.

10. Press.

Border Treatment by Lois Thornhill

Yardage for Four Blocks and Four Corner Stars

 Background . . . . . ½ yd

 First dark . . . . . . ⅓ yd

 Second dark . . . . ⅜ yd

 Second medium . . . ⅛ yd

 First light medium . . ¼ yd

Make four

Make four

Additional Yardage for Quilt

Background . . . . ⅔ yd

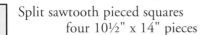 Split sawtooth pieced squares
four 10½" x 14" pieces

First dark . . . . ⅔ yd

 Split sawtooth pieced squares
four 10½" x 14" pieces

Second medium . . . . ⅝ yd

 Center of split sawtooth
four 2¼" wide strips

Outer border
four 2½" wide strips

Binding . . . . ⅜ yd

 four 3" wide strips

Backing . . . . 1¼ yds

Batting . . . . 45" square

41" x 41"

Making Pieced Squares for Split Sawtooth Border

See Grid Method, page 6.

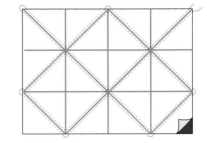

1. Use the background and dark 10½" x 14" pieces to draw a 3 x 4 grid of 3½" squares.

2. Sew, cut and square 88 pieced squares to 2¾".

Making Four Sawtooth Border Strips

1. Set aside eight pieced squares.

2. Make four stacks of 20 squares each. Turn stacks as shown.

3. Flip and sew 20 pairs of each.

4. Lay out five pairs in each row, and sew together. Sew a square to the end of each row.

Make four rows of each.

5. Cut the 2¼" wide center strips to four strips the size of your quilt center, approximately 24½" long strips.

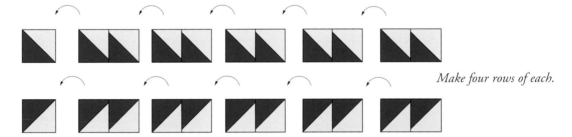

6. Pin and sew sawtooth rows to center strip. Adjust one or more seams to make rows fit the center strip. The width of the sewn together strips should be 6½" or the size of the corner star.

Adding the Sawtooth Borders and Corner Stars

1. Lay out quilt center, border pieces and star corners.

2. Sew left and right pieced borders to quilt.

3. Sew a star block to the end of the top and bottom pieced borders. Sew to quilt.

4. Sew 2½" outer border strips to quilt.

Seminole Star

The domestic resourcefulness of the Seminole women contributed much to the welfare of their people, especially when they were moved from their original homelands in Georgia and Alabama to the Florida Everglades. The Seminole Indians changed from making traditional clothing of buckskin and leather to loose-fitting cotton garments more suitable for the humid climate. Contact with American settlers and runaway slaves added to their knowledge of sewing techniques, and in 1896, the railroad brought an innovation the Seminole women were quick to take advantage of — the hand-cranked sewing machine. They evolved the technique known as Seminole patchwork, which was the first patchwork method designed especially for the sewing machine. The Seminole women sewed in groups, naming their patterns for natural elements such as lightning, rain, trees, and animals. Pictured is the wife of Billy Bowlegs, a Seminole chief from the 1800's.

Cutting Instructions

Layer cut right sides together:

 one 4½" square second medium
one 4½" square second light medium

Cut:

 one 4¾" square first dark or "fussy cut"

 one 7½" square background
one 9" square second dark

four 3½" squares background

Suggested values: choose the background, two darks, a medium, and a light medium.

Making Four Flying Geese Patches

1. Right sides together, center the 7½" square on the 9" square.

2. Sew, following Flying Geese method, page 8.

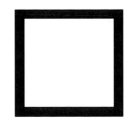

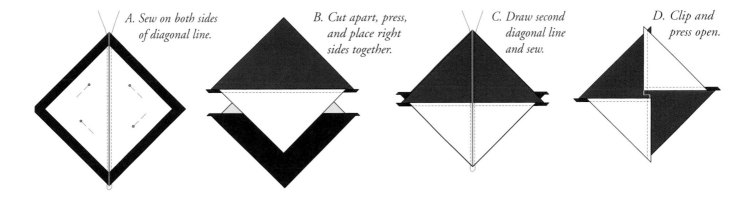

A. Sew on both sides of diagonal line.

B. Cut apart, press, and place right sides together.

C. Draw second diagonal line and sew.

D. Clip and press open.

3. Trim out four 3½" x 6½" Flying Geese patches.

Making the Center

1. Press the 4½" squares right sides together. Draw diagonal lines on the back of the lighter square. Pin.

2. Sew ¼" away from the left side of the line, across the middle, and down the right side ¼" from the line. Press.

3. Repeat sewing on the left, across the middle, and down the right side of the line.

4. Cut on lines. Open and press seams to darker fabric.

5. Mark the middle of each side of the 4¾" center square. Lay out triangles with square.

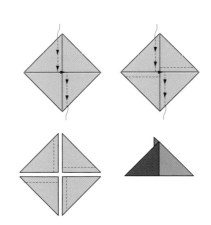

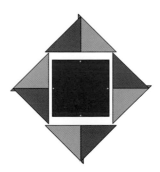

6. Flip the square to the left triangle matching the seam to marked middle. Sew ¼" seam. Add opposite side triangle. Press seams toward center.

7. Add remaining triangles. Press seams away from center.

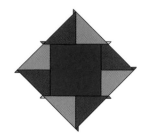

8. Square to 6½" with points of square at 3¼".

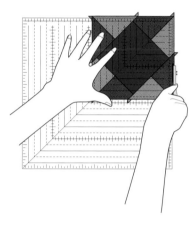

Sewing the Block Together

1. Lay out the patches.

2. Flip the middle row to the left and line up the Flying Geese peak with the seam of the center square. Assembly-line sew the vertical row.

3. Open and add the right row.

4. Sew the horizontal seams, pushing the seams in opposite directions away from the corners and center square.

5. Press.

Border Treatment by Cheryl Minshew

Yardage for Four Blocks

Background . . . . . . ½ yd

First dark . . . . ¼ yd

Second dark . . . . . . ⅓ yd

Second medium . . . . ¼ yd

Second light medium . ¼ yd

Make four

Additional Yardage for Quilt

Background . . . . ½ yd

Lattice
two 3" wide strips
Border
four 1¾" wide strips

First dark . . . . ⅔ yd

Center Square
one 3" square
Seminole border
eight 1¾" wide strips
two 4½" squares (cut on diagonal)

Second dark . . . . ⅔ yd

Center star
four 2¼" squares
eight 1¾" squares
Seminole border
eight 1¾" wide strips
two 5" squares (cut on diagonal)

Second medium . . . . . ⅔ yd

Center star
two 2¼" squares
Seminole border
eight 1¾" wide strips
Framing border
four 1¼" wide strips

36" x 36"

Second light medium . . . ½ yd

Center star
two 2¼" squares
Seminole border
nine 1" wide strips

Binding . . . . ½ yd

five 3" wide strips

Backing . . . . 1¼ yds

Batting . . . . 45" square

Making the Center Star

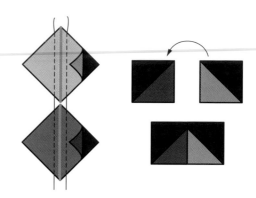

1. Mark a diagonal line on the wrong side of two 2¼" squares each of medium and light medium. Place each right sides together with a second dark square.

2. Sew ¼" from diagonal lines, cut, and square to 1¾".

3. Stack squares with medium to the left and light medium to the right. Assembly-line sew.

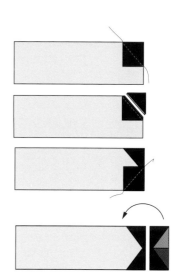

4. Cut four 12" lattice pieces from the 3" wide background strips.

5. Place 1¾" second dark squares on one end of each lattice. Mark and sew **on diagonal line**, trim, and fold out.

6. Place second square on end. Sew **on diagonal line**, trim, and fold out.

7. Assembly-line sew lattice and patches, matching seams of same fabrics.

Sewing the Top Together

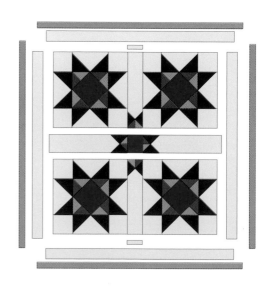

1. Lay out blocks and sew together.

2. Trim excess lattice.

3. Sew rows together and trim excess lattice.

4. Sew 1¾" wide background strips to top.

5. Sew 1¼" wide medium framing border strips to top.

Making the Seminole Border

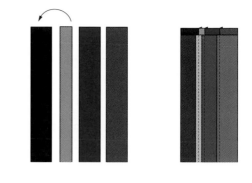

1. Sew together eight panels of strips: 1¾" second dark, 1" second light medium, 1¾" first dark, and 1¾" second medium.

2. Press seams toward medium on four panels, and away from medium on remaining four panels.

3. Place panels of opposite seam direction right sides together, locking the seams.

4. Place 45° line on ruler across top of strip. Make the first cut at a 45° angle.

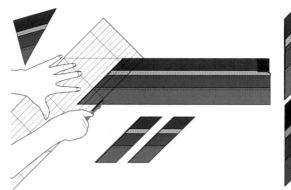

5. Move the ruler 1½" from 45° cut, and cut again. Cut a total of 60 layered pairs.

6. Sew one layered pair. Open and check that the angle is correct. Assembly-line sew a total of 60 pairs.

7. Sew 15 pairs together for each border.

8. Lay a ruler across the upper points of the narrow strip. Move it ¼" up. Trim top and lower edges, preserving ¼" seam.

Making the Border Corners

1. Assembly-line sew four first dark triangles (cut from 4½" squares) to 1" light medium strip. Leave a 2" space between triangles.

2. Sew a second dark triangle (cut from 5" squares) to opposite side. Cut apart, and press.

Adding Seminole Border

1. Lay out the quilt center, Seminole border pieces, and corners. Trim framing border if Seminole is shorter.

2. Sew the left and right side to the quilt.

3. Pin match corners and cut to size, approximately 3½" square. See white guide lines.

4. Sew a corner to each end, and add borders.

5. Cut corners on diagonal.

Harriet Beecher Stowe Star

H arriet Beecher Stowe contributed greatly to the abolitionist movement with *Uncle Tom's Cabin,* originally published as a weekly series in an antislavery paper. She had planned to write no more than three or four episodes, but the story became so popular with readers that she continued the series, eventually completing forty-five episodes in ten months. It was published in book form in 1852, and became an instant bestseller. Northerners were deeply moved by Stowe's vivid descriptions of the horrors of slavery. Her book was translated into ten languages and attracted the world's attention to the abolitionist movement.

Cutting Instructions

Layer cut right sides together:

 one 3¼" x 6½" rectangle first medium
one 3¼" x 6½" rectangle second medium

Cut:

 one 7⅜" square first dark
cut on both diagonals

 one 7¼" square background
cut on both diagonals
(discard two triangles)

 one 7½" square background
one 9" square second dark

 four 3½" squares background

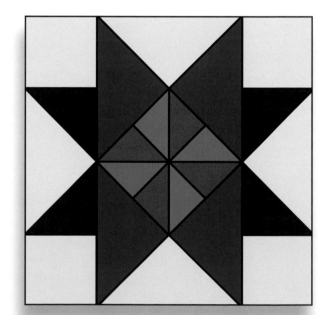

Suggested values: choose the background, two darks, and two mediums.

Making Two Flying Geese Patches

1. Right sides together, center the 7½" square on the 9" square.

2. Sew, following Flying Geese method, page 8.

3. Trim out two 3½" x 6½" Flying Geese patches.

4. Discard the two untrimmed ones.

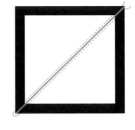

5. Lay out the corner squares and Flying Geese patches in piles of two.

6. Assembly-line sew corners to Geese patches. Press seams away from Geese.

Making the Center

1. Place the 3¼" x 6½" rectangles right sides together. Draw a 3¼" grid of two squares.

2. Sew, following Grid Method, page 6.

3. Square four patches to 2¾".

4. Lay out the four center patches.

5. Flip the right patches to the left, matching the outside edges. Assembly-line sew the vertical seam.

6. Sew the horizontal seam, pushing the seam allowances in opposite directions and locking the seams.

7. Press and square to 4¾" square.

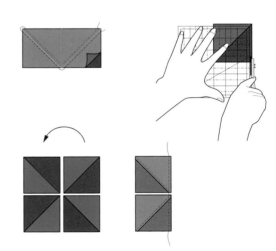

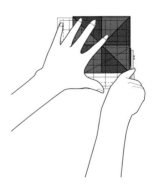

Sewing the Block Together

1. Lay out the center with dark triangles. Flip the right triangle to the center, lining up the top and right edge. Sew. Add remaining triangle. Press seams toward the triangles.

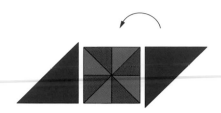

2. Lay out the dark and background triangles in piles of two. Flip and assembly-line sew. Press seams to the darker side.

3. Lay out center with pairs of triangles. Flip center to the left triangles. Match seams. Sew. Add remaining pair of triangles. Press seams away from center.

4. Trim exposed tips.

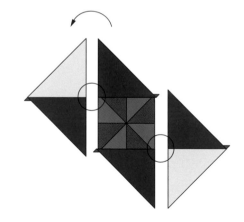

5. Lay out the center with Geese. Flip the center to the left. Pin match the meeting points. Sew.

6. Add final side. Press seams toward center.

7. Trim tips.

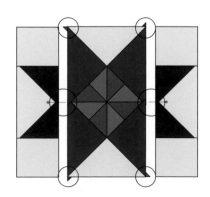

Border Treatment by LuAnn Stout

Yardage for Four Blocks

 Background . . . . . ½ yd

 First dark . . . . . . ¼ yd

 Second dark . . . ⅓ yd

 First medium . . . . ⅛ yd

 Second medium . . . ⅛ yd

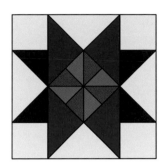

Make four

Additional Yardage for Quilt

Background . . . . 1 yd

 Corner stars
one 2" wide strip…
…sixteen 2" squares
four 3¼" squares

Triangles
one 5½" wide strip…
…four 5½" squares
(cut on diagonal)

Border
four 4½" wide strips

First dark . . . . ⅛ yd

 Corner stars
one 3" wide strip…
…eight 3" squares

Second dark . . . . . . ⅝ yd

 Corner stars
four 2" squares

Folded border
four 1½" wide strips

First medium . . . . . ⅛ yd

 Corner stars
four 3¼" squares

34" x 34"

Binding . . . . ½ yd
 four 3" wide strips

Backing . . . . 1¼ yds

Batting . . . . . . 45" square

Making the Small Corner Stars

1. Draw two diagonal lines on the wrong side of four background 3¼" squares.

2. Place marked squares with 3¼" medium squares right sides together.

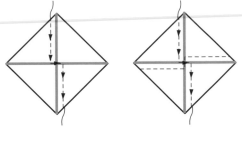

3. Sew ¼" away from the left side of the line, across the middle, and down the right side ¼" from the line. Press.

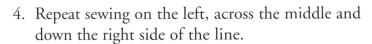

4. Repeat sewing on the left, across the middle and down the right side of the line.

5. Cut on drawn lines.

6. Press seam allowance away from the background of the sixteen pieced triangles.

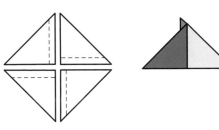

7. Stack triangles cut from 3" dark squares with sixteen pieced triangles.

8. Flip the dark triangle to the left, centering on the pieced triangle. Sew, being careful not to stretch these bias edges.

9. Press seam allowance to the dark.

10. Square to 2", being careful to have the seams end at the corners. *Line up diagonal line on ruler with diagonal seam. Place 1" square mark on cross seam. Trim two sides. Turn, and trim to perfect 2".*

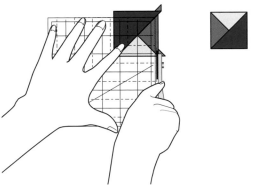

Sewing the Star Together

1. Lay out the star point squares with 2" dark and background squares.

2. Sew block together.

3. Carefully square to 4¾", preserving the ¼" seam allowance beyond the points.

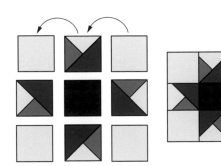

Adding Background Triangles to the Corner Stars

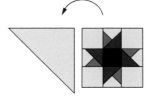

1. Stack the four stars with four triangles cut from 5½" background squares.

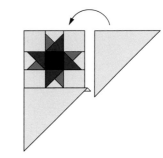

2. Flip star to triangle right sides together, matching top and right edges. Assembly-line sew stacks.

3. Press seam to triangle.

4. Sew remaining triangles.

5. Press seam to triangle, carefully avoiding long bias edge.

Adding Borders to Corner Star

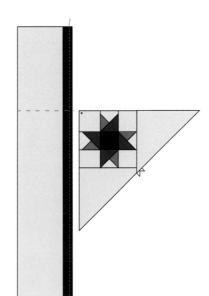

1. Fold second dark 1½" strip in half lengthwise **wrong sides together**. Press.

2. Lay folded strip on right side of 4½" background strip, matching raw edges. Sew ⅛" from raw edges.

3. Lay out sewn border and star piece. Measure down 7" from end of border.

4. Flip the star to the border. Start sewing ¼" down from the edge of the star corner in order to miter the borders. See dot on star block.

5. Open and press seam toward star and folded border toward 4½" border. Lay a 6" x 24" ruler along the long edge of the triangle, lining up 45º line on ruler. Trim off excess.

6. Use border excess for other side of star piece. Measure 7" from end of border. Pin often from dot on block to end of triangle. Sew from triangle toward block. Leave ¼" of block free where the borders meet.

7. Open and press seam toward star.

8. Place ruler across edge of triangle with 45º on edge. Trim off excess border.

9. Repeat with remaining three corner stars.

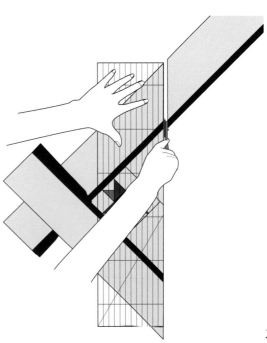

Mitering the Corners

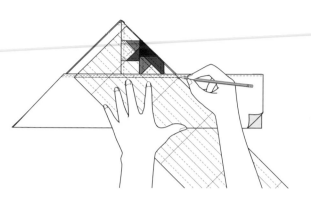

1. Fold the corner diagonally right sides together. Match the border strips, right sides together. Be sure folded border strips are matched.

2. Fingerpress seam away from border so stitching shows.

3. Line the 45° angle line of the 6" x 24" ruler with the seam of the border.

4. Following the quilt fold, draw a diagonal line on the border extension.

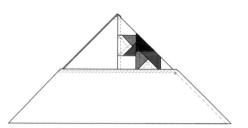

5. Start exactly at the ¼" point of stitching. Baste stitch on the drawn line.

6. Open quilt and check to see if pieces line up. If so, sew permanently. If not, press from the top to get a perfect stitching line. Sew again.

7. Repeat with remaining corners. Trim seams to ¼". Press to one side.

Sewing the Corners to the Quilt Blocks

1. Lay out the corner pieces next to the quilt top.

2. Center each corner by matching the center seams of the quilt with the point of the corner star.

3. Pin the bias edge to the quilt on opposite corners. Sew carefully, not stretching the bias edge. Fold out. Press seam toward border.

4. Sew on remaining two sides.

Barbara Frietchie Star

A bold color scheme of red and black highlights the strong geometric design of Karen's wallhanging. The background is machine-quilted in an intricate zigzag pattern. See instructions on page 13.

Karen Strausheim

Floral fabrics and spring colors make a bright and cheery wall-hanging. Lois used three ounce batting and hand quilted with white cotton thread for a tasteful finish. See instructions on page 18.

Lois Thornhill

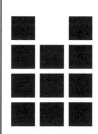

Dee made her wallhanging in country colors of pink and blue, adding an appliqued heart in the center for a winsome touch. See instructions on page 18.

Dee Brawley

Hand-embroidered violets blossom in the center squares of star blocks. The small star is formed by the lattice and triangle patches. The striking Seminole border is made from strips cut at a 45° angle. See instructions on page 23.

Linda Dahlman

The lively color scheme of Cheryl's wallhanging is a perfect complement to the strong geometric design of the Seminole border. She
added a sparkling finish with machine-quilted stars in each center
block. See instructions on page 23.

Cheryl Minshew

Harriet Beecher Stowe Star

In this elegant variation by Luann, four blocks set on point are accented by folded borders and smaller stars. The corners are mitered for a perfect finishing touch. See instructions on page 29.

LuAnn Stout

The four star blocks of Loretta's wallhanging stand out against a light lattice fabric with cornerstones. This is a perfect time-saving setting that is simple yet beautifully frames the blocks.

Loretta Smith

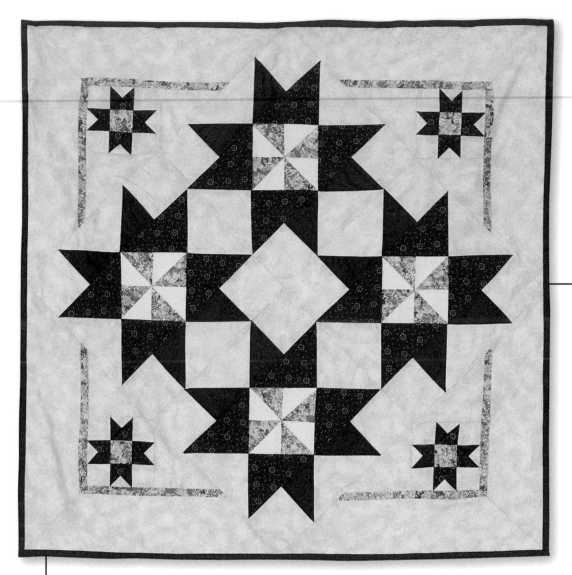

Vibrant stars of red, white, and blue leap from a cream-colored background. Ruth chose fabrics from the Benartex Documentary line to illustrate how easy it is to change the look of these versatile star blocks. See instructions on page 29.

Ruth Griffith

Pillow Treatment by Teresa Varnes

Make one Harriet Tubman Star. (See page 16.)

Additional Yardage for One Pillow

Background . . . . . . ⅓ yd

Four 2" squares
One 9" x 12" piece

First dark . . . . ⅓ yd

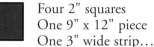
Four 2" squares
One 9" x 12" piece
One 3" wide strip…
…twelve 3" squares

Second dark . . . . ⅝ yd

One 18" square backing
Thirty-two 3" squares

Second medium . . . . ⅛ yd

Four 3½" x 9½" pieces

Pillow form . . . . 18"

Making Twenty-four Pieced Squares

See Grid Method, page 6.

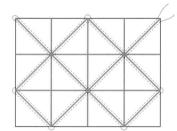

1. Place 9" x 12" rectangles right sides together. Draw a 3 by 4 grid of 3" squares.

2. Draw diagonal lines and sew ¼" away from each side.

3. Cut, press and square to 2".

Make four   *Make eight*

Making Four Corners and Eight Sides

1. Stack and sew together.

3. In stacks of four, lay out the pairs at sides of the medium 3½" x 9½" side strips.

4. Assembly-line sew to make side borders.

Finishing the Pillow

1. Lay out the pieces and sew together.

2. Make four prairie point edges, approximately 17½" long and sew to pillow front.
   Fold 3" squares in half, wrong sides together. Press and fold on second diagonal. Insert second dark folded square halfway into first folded square. Sew halfway. Insert third square into second. Sew pattern with four, three and four.

3. Pin pillow top right sides together to backing and sew around three sides. Turn right side out. Insert 18" pillow form. Stitch opening shut.

Clara Barton Star

While working as a government clerk in Washington, D.C., Clara Barton became involved in collecting and delivering supplies to northern troops who were gathered for the Civil War. She proved to have a special talent for organization, and spent the next four years delivering supplies to soldiers from both sides. Soldiers' families and local aid societies donated money and provisions, which Clara delivered in wagons borrowed from the army. When the war ended, Clara's belief that an army medical corps should be neutral led her to work for the International Red Cross. In 1881 she founded a branch of the Red Cross in the United States.

Cutting Instructions

Layer cut right sides together:

 one 4" square first dark
one 4" square first medium

 one 4" square first dark
one 4" square second medium

 one 4½" x 9" rectangle background
one 4½" x 9" rectangle second dark

Cut:

 two 4¼" squares first medium
do not cut into triangles

 two 4¼" squares second medium
do not cut into triangles

 four 3½" squares background

Suggested values: choose the background, two darks, and two mediums.

Making Two of Each

1. Place pairs of 4" squares **right sides** together. Draw diagonal lines.

2. Sew, following Grid Method, page 6.

3. Square to 3½".

Making Two of Each

1. Use the 4½" x 9" rectangles right sides together. Draw a 4½" grid, sew, and cut apart.

2. Press the four patches open, but do not square.

3. On the wrong side of each patch, draw a diagonal line crossing the seam. Use a ruler line on the seam to ensure a right angle as the square may not be true.

4. Right sides together, place marked squares on solid 4¼" squares. The solid square may be slightly larger. Press and pin each.

5. Sew ¼" on both sides of the marked diagonal line.

6. Press. Cut on the diagonal line.

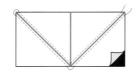

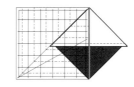

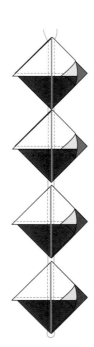

7. Press seam allowance to the large triangle.

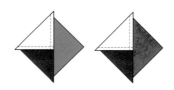

8. Place 6" ruler's diagonal line on long diagonal seam. Position the ruler's 3½" (the edge of the ruler) marks on the short seam. Trim two exposed edges. Turn patch. Position ruler's 3½" lines on the newly cut edges. The diagonal line should be on the long seam. Trim remaining edges, squaring to 3½".

Making Two of Each

1. Using the first medium fabric, lay out the pieced squares with the corner square.

2. Flip the squares on the right to the left, and assembly-line sew the vertical seam of each quarter.

3. Sew the horizontal seams, pushing the seams in opposite directions, and toward the corner square.

4. Repeat, sewing quarters using the second medium fabric. Sew the horizontal seams, pushing seams in opposite directions, and away from the corners.

5. Press the final seam of the four quarters away from the corner square so they lock when sewn together. The quarters should measure 6½" square.

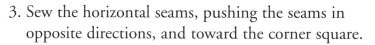
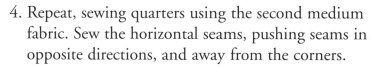
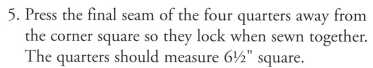

Sewing the Block Together

1. Lay out the quarters.

2. Flip the quarters on the right to the left.

3. Sew the vertical seam, matching and locking seams.

4. Sew the horizontal seam, pushing the center seams in opposite directions.

5. Press lightly on the wrong side to start seams in the desired direction. Press on the right side.

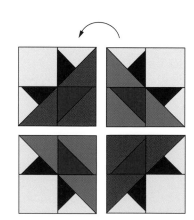

Border Treatment by Kathy Schaeffer

Yardage for Six Blocks and Twelve Quarters

 Background . . . . . 1⅛ yds

 First dark . . . . . . ½ yd

 Second dark . . . . ½ yd

 First medium . . . . ⅔ yd

 Second medium . . . ⅝ yd

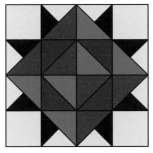

Make four

Make eight

Make six

Additional Yardage for Quilt

Background . . . . ⅝ yd

 Border pieced squares
    one 6" wide strip…
        …three 6" x 12" pieces

First border
    four 2½" wide strips

First dark . . . . ¾ yd

 Lattice
    three 2" wide strips…
        …nine 2" x 12½" pieces

Lattice cornerstones
    one 5" x 7½" piece

Border pieced squares
    one 6" x 12" piece

Second border
    three 2½" wide strips

Second dark . . . . . . ¾ yd

 Lattice
    three 2" wide strips…
        …eight 2" x 12½" pieces

Lattice cornerstones
    one 5" x 7½" piece

Border pieced squares
    one 6" x 12" piece

Third border
    three 2½" wide strips

40" x 54"

Second medium . . . . ¼ yd

 Border pieced square
    one 6" x 12" piece

Binding . . . . ½ yd

 five 3" wide strips

Backing . . . . 1¾ yds

Batting . . . . 45" x 60"

Making Six Blocks and Twelve Quarters

1. Cut and sew pieces for ten blocks. Sew six blocks together. Leave parts for four blocks in pieces.

2. Reduce the size of each quarter by squaring each 3½" patch to 2½".

3. Sew together quarters.

4. Use the remaining parts for a label on the back of the quilt.

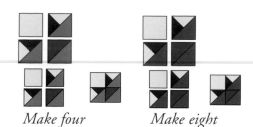

Make four   *Make eight*

Making the Lattice Cornerstones

1. Use the first dark and second dark 5" x 7½" pieces. Draw a 2 x 3 grid of 2½" squares.

2. Sew, following Grid Method, **page 6**.

3. Square the twelve pieced squares to 2".

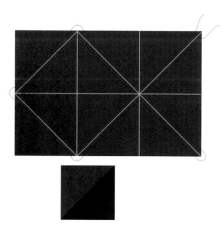

Sewing the Quilt Top Together

1. Lay out six star blocks, twelve pieced cornerstones, and nine first dark and eight second dark 2" x 12½" lattice (or your block size lattice) turned for a consistent pattern.

2. Sew the vertical seams.

3. Sew the horizontal seams.

4. Add the first border 2½" wide background strips to left and right sides.

5. Add first border strips to top and bottom.

Making Pieced Squares for the Second and Third Borders

1. Draw 2 x 4 grids of 3" squares on the back of three 6" x 12" background pieces. Pair a marked background right sides together with same size pieces of first dark, second dark and second medium pieces.

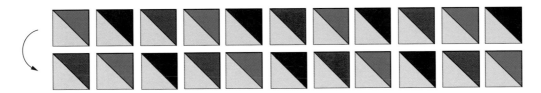

2. Sew, following Grid Method, page 6.

3. Square 16 first dark pieced squares and 14 each of second medium and second dark to 2½" square.

4. Lay out pieced squares in eleven pairs, staggering the first dark, second medium and second dark colors.

5. Repeat sewing a second set.

Adding the Second and Third Borders

1. Sew three pairs of second and third border strips.

2. Cut one pair in half to use on the left and right sides.

3. Use remaining two full sets for top and bottom.

4. Lay out quilt center with star quarters, pieced square sets and border strips.

5. Sew a darker star quarter to a pieced set.

6. Add "too long" second/third border strip.

7. Trim to fit by measuring star quarter against border strip. Overlap ½" then trim. Sew quarter to strip.

8. Sew the left and right side borders to the quilt.

9. Add the top and bottom borders, trimming by the same method.

Sojourner Truth Star

She was born a slave named Isabella. When she was emancipated at the age of forty, she chose the name Sojourner Truth to describe her mission as a traveling preacher. Speaking at religious revival meetings in the New England area, she soon gained recognition for her forceful presence and fiery lectures. Many of the leading abolitionists and women's rights activists of the time received her support and counted her as a friend. Sojourner was a gifted orator who was not afraid to speak before an unfriendly crowd. Her famous speech, "Ain't I a Woman?" brought the house down at a Women's Rights Convention in 1851, and copies were widely distributed. In her later years, Sojourner traveled all over the United States, spoke before Congress, and met two presidents.

Cutting Instructions

Layer cut right sides together:

one 6" square first medium
one 6" square second medium

Cut:

one 7¼" square first dark
    cut on both diagonals

two 3⅞" squares second dark
    cut on one diagonal

one 7¼" square background
    cut on both diagonals

four 3½" squares background

Suggested values: choose the background, two darks, and two mediums.

Making the Center

1. Press 6" squares right sides together.

2. Draw diagonal line.

3. Sew ¼" seam on both sides of drawn line. Press.

4. Cut on **unmarked** diagonal, then on marked line.

5. Press seams to darker fabric.

6. Pair two pieces and discard rest.

7. Sew right sides together. Press.

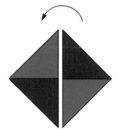

8. **Square to 4¾".**

   Place 6" ruler on square. Line up 2⅜" square point on ruler with center of block. Trim two sides, turn, and square to 4¾".

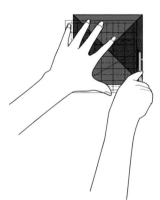

Making Four

1. Stack corner squares and second dark triangles cut from 3⅞" squares.

2. Flip square to triangle right sides together. Match the top and right edges. Assembly-line sew stacks. Press seam to background square.

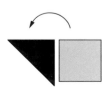

3. Stack sewn pieces with first dark triangles from 7¼" square.

4. Flip dark triangle to sewn piece, matching triangle edges. Assembly-line sew stacks.

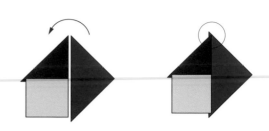

5. Press seam allowance away from large triangle.

6. Trim circled tip on all four.

Sewing the Block Together

1. Lay out sewn pieces with background triangles cut from 7¼" square.

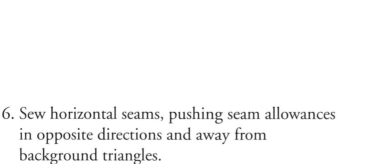

2. Flip the middle row to the left. Match tips and square bottoms.

3. Sew vertical seam, matching the right edges and square corners.

4. Open and check for seam allowance.

5. Add right row.

6. Sew horizontal seams, pushing seam allowances in opposite directions and away from background triangles.

7. Press seam allowances away from center.

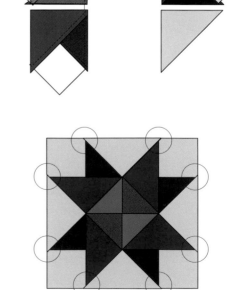

Border Treatment by Sheila Meehan

Yardage for Five Blocks

 Background   . . ⅔ yd

 First dark   . . . ¼ yd

 Second dark   . . ¼ yd

 First medium   . . ¼ yd

 Second medium   . ¼ yd

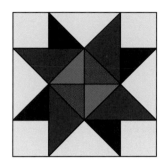

Make five

Additional Yardage for Quilt

Background . . . . . . 1 yd

 Four corners
    two 9½" squares (cut on diagonal)
Four sides
    one 18" square (cut on both diagonals)

Ribbon border
    two 4½" wide strips…
      …twelve 4½" squares
    two 4" squares

First dark . . . . . . ⅝ yd

 Folded border
    four 1" wide strips
Ribbon border
    three 4¼" wide strips…
     … twenty-four 4¼" squares
      (cut on diagonal)

Second dark . . . . . . ⅓ yd

Ribbon border
    two 4½" wide strips…
     …twelve 4½" squares
    two 4" squares

Second medium . . . . ¼ yd

Border
    four 1¾" wide strips

Binding . . . . ½ yd

 five 3" wide strips

43" x 43"

Backing . . . . 1¼ yds

Batting . . . . 48" square

Adding Background Triangles

1. Lay out five blocks, corner triangles and side triangles.

2. Sew the smaller corner triangles to the adjacent blocks.

3. Sew pieces of each row.

4. Sew rows together.

5. Square up the raw edges of the set triangles. Be sure to leave a ¼" seam allowance.

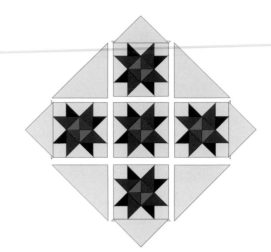

Adding the Folded Border

1. Fold in half and press each 1" wide strip **wrong sides together**.

2. Lay folded edge toward stars, matching raw edges.

3. Sew strips to left and right sides. Trim to fit. Increase stitch length and sew with an ⅛" seam allowance.

4. Sew top and bottom strips. Trim to fit.

Adding Second Border

1. Sew left and right 1¾" strips to quilt.

2. Sew top and bottom strips to quilt.

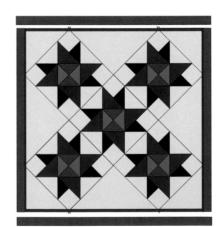

Making the Ribbon Border

1. Draw two diagonal lines on the wrong side of twelve 4½" background squares. Place each right sides together with a second dark 4½" square.

2. Sew ¼" away from the left side of the line, across the middle, and down the right side ¼" from the line. Press.

3. Repeat sewing on the left, across the middle and down the right side of the line.

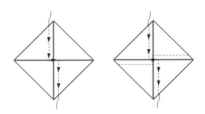

4. Cut on drawn lines.

5. Press open 48 pieced triangles, seam to the dark fabric.

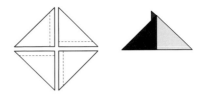

6. Stack 48 pieced triangles with dark triangles cut from (24) 4¼" squares. Flip the pieced triangle to the dark triangle. Assembly-line sew stacks.

7. Square each evenly to 3½", with seams ending in the corners.

8. In stacks of 24, lay out the squares to form the pattern. Assembly-line sew stacks into pairs.

9. Sew six pairs together for each side of quilt.

10. Sew ribbon borders to left and right sides of quilt.

11. Ribbon border corners: Draw a diagonal line on the wrong side of two 4" background squares. Pair each with dark square. Sew ¼" from both sides of line. Cut on line, press open, and square four pieced squares to 3½".

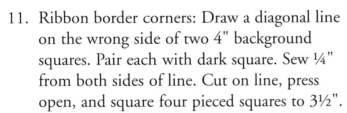

12. Sew a corner square to each end of the top and bottom ribbon borders. Sew to quilt.

Jane Addams Star

Jane Addams was a well-to do young woman who became a social reformer in response to the urban problems of overcrowding, poverty, and disease she observed in the slums of Chicago. Hull House was founded in 1891, and became a haven for the immigrants who lived and worked in the surrounding tenements. Settlement workers helped them obtain medical care, education, food, and employment at a time when no government programs were in place to help them. Hull House offered day-care in the form of kindergarten and after-school clubs, while adults took classes in nutrition and household management, attended lectures, and held union meetings.

Cutting Instructions

Layer cut right sides together:

one 2⅝" x 6" strip second light medium
one 2⅝" x 6" strip first dark

Cut:

two 3⅞" squares first dark
   cut on one diagonal

one 7¼" square second dark
   cut on both diagonals

four 2⅝" squares second medium
two 4¼" squares background
   cut on both diagonals

four 3½" squares background

Suggested values: *choose the background, two darks, a medium, and a light medium.*

Making the Center

1. Sew 6" strips right sides together. Press seam allowance to darker fabric.

2. Trim end and cut two 2⅝" pieces.

3. Lay out pieces, flip together and sew.

4. Patchwork should measure 4¾".

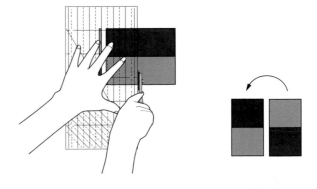

Making Four

1. Flip triangles cut from 3⅞" squares to background squares, right sides together.

2. Match top and right edges. Assembly-line sew. Press seam allowance to background square.

3. Stack sewn pieces with dark triangles from 7¼" square.

4. Flip sewn piece to triangle, matching triangle edges. Assembly-line sew stacks.

5. Press seam away from large triangle. Trim circled tip.

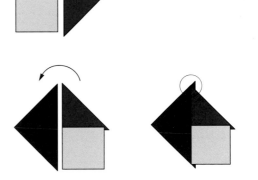

Making Four

1. Flip four 2⅝"squares to four background triangles cut from 4¼" squares. Match top and right edges, and sew. Press seam to triangle.

2. Lay out stack of sewn pieces with remaining four background triangles.

3. Flip and sew. Press seam to triangle.

Sewing the Block Together

1. Lay out sewn pieces.

2. Flip middle row to the left, matching tips. Match right edges and square corners. Sew.

3. Open and add right row.

4. Sew horizontal rows, pushing seam allowances in opposite directions and away from center.

5. Press seam allowances away from center.

Border Treatment by Pat Wetzel

Yardage for Four Blocks

Background . . . . ½ yd

First dark . . . . . . ¼ yd

Second dark . . . . . ¼ yd

Second medium . . . . ¼ yd

Second light medium . . ⅛ yd

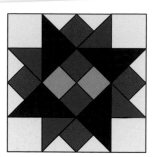

Make four

Additional Yardage for Quilt

Background . . . . ½ yd

Corners for center
one 3" square (cut on both diagonals)
Pinwheel
two 6" x 12" pieces

Second border
three 2½" wide strips

First dark . . . . ⅔ yd

Pinwheel
two 6" x 12" pieces
Lattice
two 2½" wide strips...
... four 2½" x size of your block

First border
four 2½" wide strips

Second medium . . . . ⅓ yd

Center
one 1⅞" square
Third border
three 2½" wide strips

Binding . . . . ½ yd

four 3" wide strips

38" x 38"

Backing . . . . 1¼ yds

Batting . . . . 45" square

Making the Center

1. Sew corner triangles cut from 3" square to 1⅞" center.

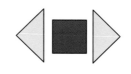
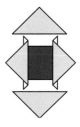

2. Square to 2½".

Making the Second and Third Border Strips

1. Sew three pairs of second and third border strips.

2. Cut eight paired pieces at the size of your block plus 1", approximately 13½".

Making the Pinwheels

1. Draw a 3" grid on the 6" x 12" pieces.

2. Sew, following Grid Method, page 6.

3. Cut, and square 32 pieced squares to 2½".

4. Stack and sew together eight pinwheels, pushing seams in opposite directions toward the dark.

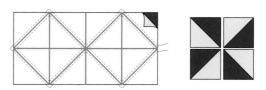

Sewing the Quilt Top Together

1. Lay out and sew together the four blocks, four lattice pieces and center.

2. Measure top, cut and sew first border pieces.

3. Lay out quilt center, pinwheels and border strips.

4. Sew a pinwheel between all side border strips.

5. Sew left and right borders to quilt.

6. Add pinwheels to ends of top and bottom.

7. Sew to quilt.

Susan B. Anthony Star

Susan B. Anthony was an organizer and leader of the women's rights movement in the early part of the nineteenth century. Traveling extensively, she gave lectures to women's groups and associations, including quilting circles. During this period, quilting bees provided an accepted excuse for gatherings of homebound women and were an important network for the exchange of ideas. Susan worked all her life for women's suffrage but did not live to see it before her death in 1906. On August 26, 1920, the amendment was passed, giving all women in the United States the right to vote.

Cutting Instructions

Cut:

 two 2⅝" squares second medium
one 3¼" square first light medium
one 3¼" square second medium

 one 3⅞" square first dark
cut on one diagonal

 one 3⅞" square second dark
cut on one diagonal

 one 5⅛" square first dark
cut on one diagonal

 one 5⅛" square second dark
cut on one diagonal

 one 7¼" square background
cut on both diagonals

 four 3½" squares background

Suggested values: choose the background, two darks, a medium, and a light medium.

58

Making the Center

1. Place the 3¼" squares right sides together, sew, and cut apart.

2. Square two pieced squares to 2⅝".

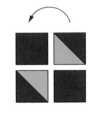

3. Lay out pieced and solid squares. Flip right squares onto left. Assembly-line sew vertical seam.

4. Sew horizontal seam, pushing seam allowances to solid squares. Press.

5. Patchwork should measure 4¾".

Making Four Different Corners

1. Lay out triangles cut from 3⅞" squares with corner squares.

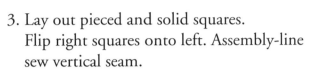

2. Flip the piece on the right to the left, and line up straight edges. Assembly-line sew.

3. Press seam allowances to background squares.

4. Lay out triangles cut from 5⅛" squares. Place sewn pieces so that opposite fabrics will be sewn together.

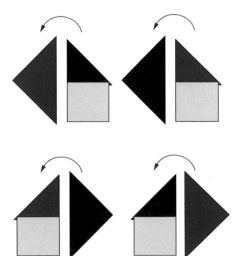

5. Flip the piece on the right to the left, matching right edges and triangles. A ⅜" tip must extend below square.

6. Assembly-line sew.

7. Set and press seam allowances away from large triangle. Trim circled tip.

Sewing the Block Together

1. Lay out sewn pieces with background triangles cut from 7¼" square. Make sure pieces form pattern.

2. Flip the middle row to the left. Match tips.

3. Sew vertical seam, matching the right edges and square corners.

4. Open and add right row.

5. Sew horizontal seams, pushing seam allowances in opposite directions and away from background triangles.

6. Press seam allowances away from center.

7. Square the block to 12½", or your average block size.

Border Treatment by Dee Brawley

Yardage for Four Blocks

 Background . . . . ½ yd

 First dark . . . . . ¼ yd

 Second dark . . . ¼ yd

 Second medium . . ⅛ yd

 First light medium . ⅛ yd

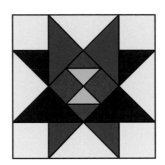

Make Four

Additional Yardage for Quilt

Background . . . . ½ yd

 Border pieced triangle squares
two 7½" x 10" pieces
Border triangles
three 2½" wide strips…
…forty-eight 2½" squares
(cut on one diagonal)

First dark . . . . ¾ yd

 Lattice
four 3" wide strips

Outer lattice
four 2" wide strips…
… eight 2" x size of your block
…twelve 3" x 2" pieces
…four 2" squares

Second dark . . . . . . ½ yd

Border large triangles
two 4" wide strips…
…twenty-four 4" squares
(cut on one diagonal)
Border corner triangles
two 6" squares (cut on one diagonal)

First light medium . . . ½ yd

 Star cornerstones
one 3" wide strip…
…nine 3" squares
Lattice star points
one 8" x 33" piece

41" x 41"

Second light medium . . ¼ yd

 Border pieced triangle squares
two 7½" x 10" pieces

Binding . . . . ½ yd

 four 3" wide strips

Backing . . . . 1¼ yds

Batting . . . . 48" square

Cutting the Lattice

1. Measure the size of your block. Add ⅛" to that measurement to compensate for shrinkage after sewing on star points.

2. Cut twelve lattice (block size plus ⅛") from the 3" wide strips.

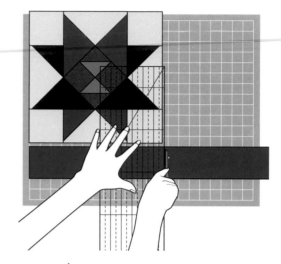

Marking the Star Squares

1. Draw a 4 x 18 grid of 1¾" squares on the wrong side of the 8" x 33" piece of star point fabric.

2. Draw a diagonal line across each square.

3. Cut into 72 marked squares.

Making Twelve Star Point Lattice

1. Place a 1¾" square right sides together to the lattice, carefully lining up the outside edges.

2. Assembly-line sew **on the diagonal line**, overlapping the top of the new lattice each time.

3. Turn the lattice around and assembly-line sew a second square to each lattice.

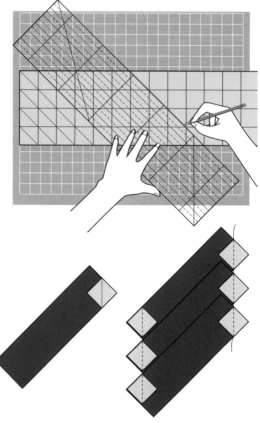

4. Trim seams to ¼" from diagonal line on both sides and press the star points flat.

5. Assembly-line sew 1¾" squares to the remaining two corners.

6. Trim seams to ¼" and press the star points flat.

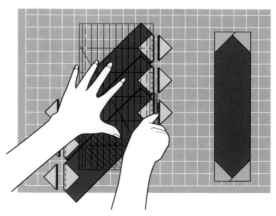

Making the Outer Star Point Lattice

1. Assembly-line sew 1¾" star square to each 3" x 2" lattice piece. Trim and press open.

2. Add star point to other side of each piece.

3. Trim and press open.

Sewing the Quilt Top Together

1. Lay out blocks, 3" star cornerstones, and 3" wide star point lattice.

2. Sew vertical seams.

3. Sew horizontal seams.

4. For left and right sides of quilt, sew three star point pieces with two 2" lattice pieces, cut to the size of your block.
Sew to sides.

5. Repeat for top and bottom, adding 2" square to each end. Sew to top and bottom of quilt.

Making Eight Border Strips

1. Use the two 7½" x 10" pieces of background and second light medium for the grid method. Draw a 3 x 4 grid of 2½" squares on the back of the background pieces.

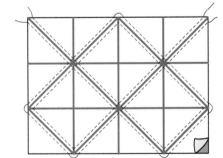

2. Sew, following Grid Method, page 6.

3. Square forty-eight pieced squares to 2".

4. In stacks of forty-eight, lay 2" pieced squares with background triangles cut from 2½" squares. Flip and sew triangle to square.

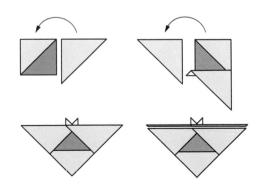

5. Add a second triangle to square. Trim pieced triangle, leaving ¼" seam allowance.

4. Lay out stacks of forty-eight pieced triangles with dark triangles cut from 4" squares. Flip and center pieced triangle on solid triangle. Sew.

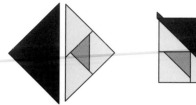

5. Square to 3½".

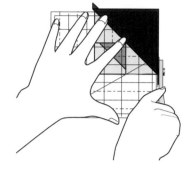

Adding the Pieced Border

1. Sew together six border squares and another six in mirror image. Repeat for each edge of quilt.

   These strips are longer than each side.

2. Sew strips to the left and right sides, **centering strips on quilt.** Trim excess.

3. Sew remaining strips to top and bottom.

4. Sew an oversized triangle, cut from 6" squares, to each corner so that its seam will cross background triangle points.

5. Trim oversized triangle to square corner of quilt.

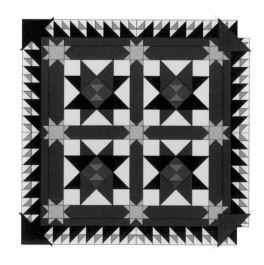

Clara Barton Star

Triangle-pieced stars sparkle in brilliant turquoise and amethyst fabrics, while pieced squares in the lattice give the illusion of mitered corners. Cornerstone stars are miniatures of the featured star. See instructions on page 45.

Kathy Schaeffer

Clara Barton Star

Lois used antique red, colonial green, and black to give her quilt an old-fashioned look. The fabrics are from the Documentaries line of Benartex. See instructions on page 45.

Lois Thornhill

Sojourner Truth Star

A ribbon border made from assembly-line sewn triangles frames five blocks on point, while a small folded border adds an extra touch of color. Sheila machine-quilted the triangle backgrounds using a stencil pattern. See instructions on page 51.

Sheila Meehan

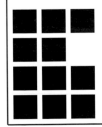

Sojourner Truth Star

A delicate Silk Floral fabric from Benartex accents the strong geometrics of the ribbon border, made even more striking in purple and gold. The narrow folded border repeats the regal color of the binding. See instructions on page 51.

Sue Bouchard

Jane Addams Star

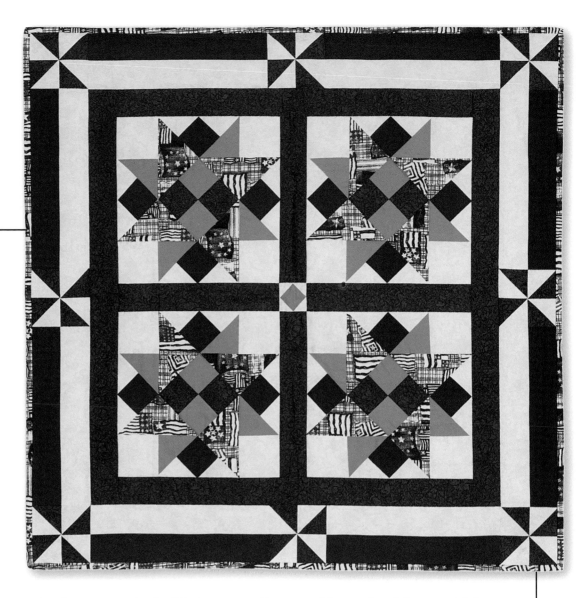

A cheery patriotic fabric, complimented by red, white, and blue borders, is perfect for the Fourth of July. Pinwheel patches of blue and white accent the lattice and cornerstone border. See instructions on page 56.

Pat Wetzel

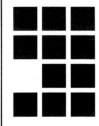

Classic fabrics from the Benartex Woodlands line give Sheila's wallhanging a rich and traditional look. The pieced stars are placed upon a Mayflower muslin print, also from Benartex. See instructions on page 56.

Sheila Meehan

Susan B. Anthony Star

A lattice in a lovely Benartex floral, with star points in a golden marbled fabric, create a softer composition for this wallhanging. The border is dramatic in hunter green and mauve, repeating the colors of the star blocks. See instructions on page 61.

Annitte Hester

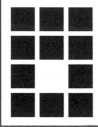

Four star blocks are framed in a lattice tipped with star points in this variation by Dee Brawley. The outer border is made of triangle patches in a fascinating mirror image design. See instructions on page 61.

Dee Brawley

Planning a Flying Geese Border for Any Size Quilt

Sue Bouchard designed this variation of the Harriet Tubman Star. In place of the background corners, she made four miniaturized blocks. To make the block between the miniaturized blocks the same size, she added a strip and Flying Geese to the large patch.

1. Set your quilt top together.

2. Measure a side. Subtract ½" seam allowance to determine finished length. If it measures an odd length, add a narrow framing border to bring it up to an even whole number.

In this example, Geese need to fit next to a 6½" patch.

$$\begin{array}{r} 6\tfrac{1}{2}" \\ -\ \tfrac{1}{2}" \\ \hline 6" \end{array}$$

3. Determine what whole numbers will divide equally into that measurement.

6" is equally divisible by 1, 2, 3, and 6.

4. The whole number selected is the height of the **finished** Geese.

For Geese in proportion to the scale of the quilt, select 1, or 1" finished height.

5. Multiply the height of the Geese x 2 for the width of the Geese.

multiply 1" x 2 for the finished width or 2".

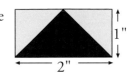

6. Divide the height of the Geese into the measurement of the side for the number of Geese.

1" goes into 6" six times.
Six Geese x four sides = twenty-four Geese.

7. Determine the size of squares to cut from the finished size of the Flying Geese patch.

Middle Triangle of the Patch
Cut a square 1½" larger than the finished width.

Middle Triangle of Patch

$$\begin{array}{r} 2" \\ +1\tfrac{1}{2}" \\ \hline 3\tfrac{1}{2}" \text{ square} \end{array}$$

End Triangles of the Patch
Cut a square 3" larger than the finished width.

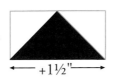

End Triangles of Patch

$$\begin{array}{r} 2" \\ +3" \\ \hline 5" \text{ square} \end{array}$$

8. A square of each produces four Flying Geese patches, or one for each side.

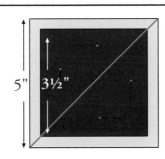

Cut: six 3½" dark squares
six 5" light squares
to make twenty-four Geese patches.

9. Sew, following Flying Geese method, page 8.

Eleanor Roosevelt Star

First Lady Eleanor Roosevelt achieved a reputation as a reformer and a humanitarian. She encouraged government programs for the poor, blacks, Native Americans, and women. As a delegate to the United Nations, she helped write the Universal Declaration of Human Rights. Quilters also remember Eleanor for her sponsorship of craft training projects under the WPA. Women were taught quilt making, applique work, weaving, and textile design in areas of Appalachia, the Carolinas and the Midwest. This renewed interest in handicrafts and quilting contributed greatly to the quilting "boom" of the 1930's.

Cutting Instructions

Cut:

  one 3½" square first medium

  two 3¼" squares first dark
cut on one diagonal

  four 2¼" x 5" strips first dark
one 7¼" square second medium
cut on both diagonals

  two 3⅞" squares second dark
cut on one diagonal

  one 7¼" square background
cut on both diagonals

  four 3½" squares background

Suggested values: choose the background, two darks, and two mediums.

Making the Center

1. Lay out the 3½" medium center square with triangles cut from 3¼" dark squares.

2. Flip square to the left triangle, right sides together. Sew ¼" seam.

3. Add opposite side triangle. Press seam allowances away from square.

4. Add remaining triangles. Press seam allowances away from square.

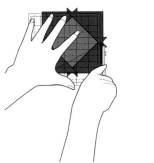

5. Square block to 4¾". Center ruler at 2⅜".

Making Four

1. Stack the four triangles cut from the medium 7¼" square. Measure up 2" from base. Cut away upper part and discard.

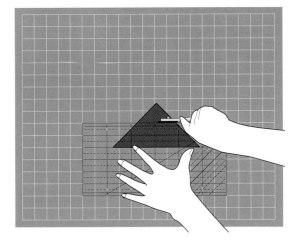

2. Stack 2" triangle bases with 2¼" x 5"strips. Flip and center the base right sides together to strip. Assembly-line sew.

3. Press seam allowance to triangle base. Avoid pressing bias edges.

4. Lay ruler on sewn piece matching ruler edges with triangle edges.

5. Trim strip to form triangle.

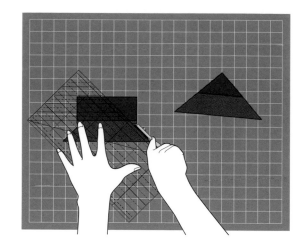

Making Four

1. Stack and lay out corner squares with triangles cut from 3⅞" squares. Flip triangle to square, and assembly-line sew.

2. Press seam allowances to background square.

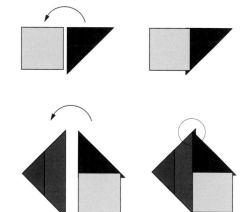

3. Stack and lay out sewn pieces with pieced triangle. Flip corner piece to triangle, matching triangle edges. Assembly-line sew.

4. Press seam allowances away from large triangle.

5. Trim circled tip.

Sewing the Block Together

1. Lay out sewn pieces with background triangles cut from 7¼" square.

2. Flip center row onto the left. Assembly-line sew vertical seam matching right edges and square corners. Match the point of the center square with the seam on the large triangle.

3. Open and add right row.

4. Sew horizontal rows, pushing seams in opposite directions and away from background triangles.

5. Press seam allowances away from center.

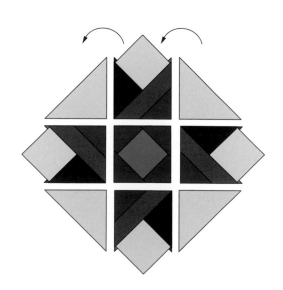

Border Treatment by Sue Bouchard

Yardage for Six Blocks

 Background . . ⅔ yd

 First dark . . . ½ yd

 Second dark . . ¼ yd

 First medium . . ⅛ yd

Second medium . ½ yd

Make six

Additional Yardage for Quilt

Background . . . . . . 2 yds

 Flying Geese
>   three 7" wide strips…
>   …twelve 7" squares
>   two 5½" wide strips…
>   …eight 5½" squares

Lattice
>   seven 2½" wide strips…
>   …seventeen 2½" x size of
>   your block
>   …sixteen 2½" squares
>   …two 2½" x 4½" pieces

Outside border
>   four 2½" wide strips
Chevron corners
>   four 4½" squares

First dark . . . . 1 yd

 Flying Geese
>   two 7" wide strips…
>   …eight 7" squares
>   two 5½" wide strips…
>   …twelve 5½" squares

Chevron corners
>   one 2½" wide strip…
>   …sixteen 2½" squares

Second dark . . . . . . ½ yd

 Folded border
>   ten 1¼" wide strips

42" x 56"

Binding . . . . ½ yd

five 3" wide strips

Backing . . . . 1⅔ yds

Batting . . . . 48" x 60"

77

Making the Flying Geese Patches

1. Center the 5½" squares on the 7" squares.

2. Sew, following Flying Geese method, page 8.

3. Trim out four 2½" x 4½" Flying Geese patches from each set. You need 48 dark Geese patches and 32 light Geese patches.

Make twelve sets   *Make eight sets*

48   32

Making the Chevron Sides with Folded Border

1. Stack 32 light and 32 dark Flying Geese. Sew 32 pairs.

2. Assembly-line sew four sets of five chevrons.

3. Sew two dark Flying Geese patches so the points meet in the middle.

4. Sew this pair between sets of five. Repeat for other side border.

5. Fold and press the 1¼" wide folded border strips **wrong sides together**. Match raw edges of folded border with chevron border, and pin. Sew folded border with ⅛" seam to both sides of chevron border strip.

6. Press folded border toward the chevron.

7. Pin and sew on an outside border.

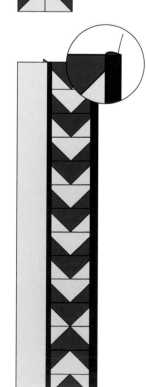

Making the Chevron Top and Bottom

1. Assembly-line sew four sets of three chevrons.

2. Sew two dark Flying Geese patches, points facing each other, with a 4½" x 2½" background fabric rectangle between them.

3. Sew this unit between sets of three. Repeat for other border.

4. Add folded borders and outside border.

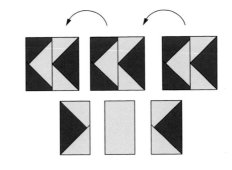

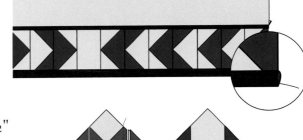

Making Four Chevron Corners

1. Right sides together, lay 2½" squares on 4½" square. Draw and sew on diagonal lines.

2. Trim ¼" from line. Press corners out.

3. Repeat on opposite corners.

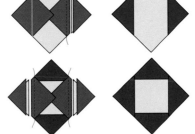

4. Sew folded borders to two opposite sides. Trim. Sew folded borders to remaining sides.

5. Assembly-line sew four chevron corners.

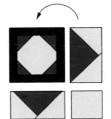

Sewing the Quilt Top Together

1. Lay out the six blocks with lattice and 2½" cornerstones. Assembly-line sew vertical rows. Sew horizontal rows.

2. Measure side chevron borders against quilt top. Trim if necessary.

3. Sew side chevrons to quilt top.

4. Sew chevron corners to top and bottom.

5. Sew borders to quilt top.

Frances Willard Star

As leader of the Women's Christian Temperance Union for twenty years, Frances Willard campaigned for a variety of social reforms related to women and children, including child labor laws, prison reform, and women's suffrage. By linking women's rights to the temperance movement, she was able to make the WCTU an effective agent for social change. Many women who would not otherwise have supported suffrage were drawn to her message of woman's role as "social housekeeper." Frances enjoyed public speaking and possessed a talent for it, becoming one of the most influential leaders of the WCTU.

Cutting Instructions

Cut:

one 7½" square background
one 9" square first dark

one 3½" square first medium or "fussy cut"

one 2¼" x 15" strip second medium
    into two 7½" strips

one 2¼" x 15" strip second dark
    into two 7½" strips

four 3½" squares background

Suggested values: choose the background, two darks, and two mediums.

Making Four Flying Geese Patches

1. Right sides together, center the 7½" square on the 9" square.

2. Sew, following Flying Geese method, page 8.

3. Trim out four 3½" x 6½" Flying Geese patches.

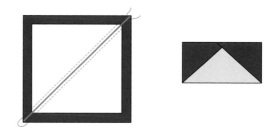

Making the Center

1. On wrong side of 3½" medium square, mark a dot ¼" from edges at each corner.

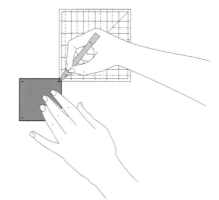

2. Right sides up, lay out 2¼" x 7½" dark and medium strips with square. Flip square to strip, centering square on strip right sides together. Pin through dots.

3. Sew from dot to dot with strip on bottom, leaving ¼" free at each end of square.

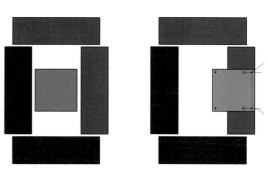

4. Lay square-with-strip right sides together on remaining medium strip. Pin through dots and sew, leaving ¼" free at each end. Avoid sewing first strip in seam.

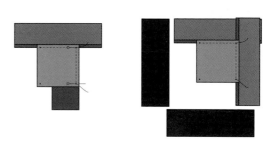

5. Add dark strips in same manner.

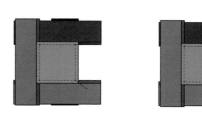

6. Fold piece in half on diagonal right sides together. Line up strips. Lay ruler's 45° line along stitching. Match ruler's right edge with dot. Mark a 45° sewing line from end of stitching to edge of strip. Pin at line through both strips.

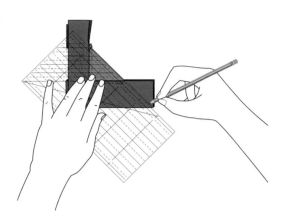

7. Sew on marked line from dot to edge of strips. Repeat with other corners.

8. Trim corner seam allowances, and press seam open. Press seam allowances away from square.

9. Place diagonal line on 12½" ruler on mitered seam. **Square to 6½" evenly.**

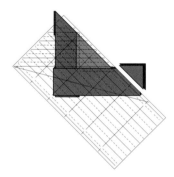

Sewing the Block Together

1. Lay out the center square, corner squares, and Flying Geese patches.

2. Flip the middle row to the left, and assembly-line sew the vertical seam.

3. Open and add the right row.

4. Sew the horizontal seams, pushing the seams in opposite directions toward Geese.

5. Press flat from the center out.

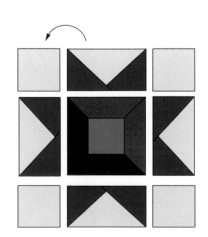

Border Treatment by Annitte Hester

Yardage for Four Blocks

 Background . . ½ yd

 First dark . . . ⅓ yd

 Second dark . . ¼ yd

 First medium . . ⅛ yd

 Second medium . ¼ yd

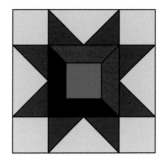

Make four

Additional Yardage for Quilt

Background . . . . . . ⅔ yd

 Flying Geese
three 7" wide strips…
…fourteen 7" squares

Second dark . . . . . . ⅝ yd

 Star block frame
four 2½" wide strips…
…eight 2½" x 18" pieces
Border square frame
three 1½" wide strips…
…sixteen 1½" x 6" pieces
Flying Geese
one 5½" wide strip…
…six 5½" squares

First medium . . . . . ½ yd

 Flying Geese
two 5½" wide strips…
…eight 5½" squares
Border square centers
eight 2½" squares

Second medium . . . . ½ yd

 Star block frame
four 2½" wide strips…
…eight 2½" x 18" pieces
Border square frame
threc 1½" wide strips…
…sixteen 1½" x 6" pieces

40" x 40"

Binding . . . . ½ yd

 four 3" wide strips

Backing . . . . 1¼ yds

Batting . . . . 48" square

Making the Frame for Star Blocks

1. Lay 2½" x 18" second medium and dark strips by block.

2. Use the same mitering technique described for block center.

3. Square to 16½".

The framed mitered lattice is also known as "attic windows."

Sewing the Quilt Top Together

1. Lay out the framed star blocks.

2. Sew the vertical seam.

3. Sew the horizontal seam.

Making Eight Border Framed Squares

1. Lay out a 2½" first medium fabric square with two 1½" x 6" strips of the second medium and two 1½" x 6½" strips of the dark.

2. Use the same mitering technique described for block center.

3. Square to 4½".

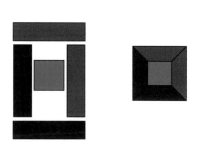

Making the Flying Geese Patches

1. Center the 5½" squares on the 7" squares.

2. Sew, following Flying Geese method, page 8.

3. Trim out four 2½" x 4½" Flying Geese patches from each set. You need 32 first medium Geese patches and 24 dark Geese patches.

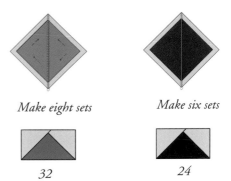

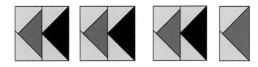

Make eight sets   *Make six sets*

32   24

4. Sew Flying Geese into eight sets of seven, alternating fabrics. Each set should begin and end with the first medium.

Adding the Pieced Border

1. Lay out quilt center with sets of Geese pointing toward corners, and border squares turned to your satisfaction.

2. Sew a border square between pairs for the left and right. Sew to quilt.

3. Sew a border square between top and bottom pairs.

4. Add the corner squares and sew to quilt.

Marie Webster Star

One of the most influential pattern designers of the 20th century, Marie Webster began her career by sending a quilt of her own design to Ladies Home Journal. Demand for her patterns was so great, she started her own business. She offered complete patterns, templates, fabric swatches, and a picture of the finished quilt — all for just fifty cents! Between 1912 and 1930, she created nineteen more original designs. After publishing *Quilts: Their Story and How to Make Them* in 1915, she was in great demand as a lecturer. She gave an informative and entertaining presentation, dressed in an Early American style green silk gown.

Her home in Marion, Indiana, has been designated a National Historic Landmark. The Quilters Hall of Fame is currently restoring the home for use as a museum.

Cutting Instructions

Cut:

one 2⅝" x 6" strip second light medium
one 2⅝" x 6" strip first dark

two 4¼" squares first medium
    cut on one diagonal

one 4½" x 9" rectangle second medium
one 4½" x 9" rectangle second dark

one 7¼" square background
    cut on both diagonals

four 3½" squares background

Suggested values: choose the background, two darks, two mediums, and a light medium.

Making the Four-Patch

1. Sew 6" strips right sides together. Press seam allowance to darker fabric.

2. Trim end and cut two 2⅝" pieces.

3. Lay out pieces. Flip together and sew, matching seams and pushing seam allowances to darker fabric.

4. Press. The four-patch should measure 4¾". The center is at 2⅜" on the ruler.

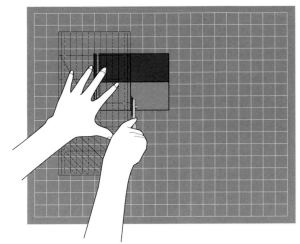

Making the Center

1. Lay out the four first medium triangles cut from 4¼" squares with four-patch. Flip four-patch to triangle. Sew.

2. Add opposite side. Press seam allowances away from four-patch.

3. Add remaining sides. Press seam allowances away from four-patch.

4. Square to 6½" with seams at 3¼".

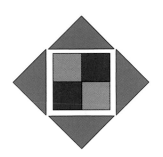

Making Four

1. Use the 4½" x 9" rectangles right sides together. Draw a 4½" grid of two squares.

2. Draw diagonal lines.

3. Sew, following Grid Method on page 6.

4. Cut apart and square each patch to 4".

5. Cut each on the diagonal, crossing the seam. Do not press bias edges.

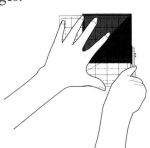

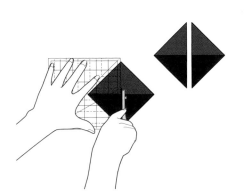

Making Four

1. In piles of four, lay out background triangles cut from 7¼" square with the pieced triangles, darker tip to base of background triangle.

2. Flip a pieced triangle to background triangle. Match bottom edge of background triangle with dark triangle. Pin and assembly-line sew a ¼" seam from top center, down to bottom edge.

3. Fingerpress top of seam to pieced triangle.

4. Add the opposite triangle. Flip large triangle to pieced triangle, matching bottom edges. Pin and sew from top center down to bottom edge.

5. Press seam allowances toward pieced triangles.

6. Carefully trim patch to 3½" x 6½", with peak centered at 3¼" and seams ending at corners. Leave ¼" seam allowance above peak.

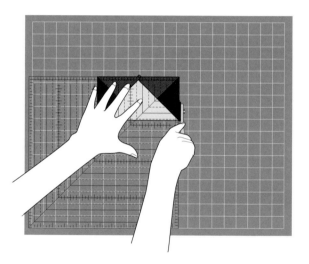

Sewing the Block Together

1. Lay out the center, corner squares, and pieced Flying Geese.

2. Flip the middle row to the right row. Carefully match seams, and sew vertical seam.

3. Open and add right row.

4. Sew horizontal seams, pushing seam allowances away from center square and away from corner squares.

5. Press horizontal seam allowances away from center.

Border Treatment by Sandy Thompson

Yardage for Four Blocks

 Background . . . . . ½ yd

 First dark . . . . . ⅛ yd

 Second dark . . . . . ¼ yd

 First medium . . . . ¼ yd

 Second medium . . . . ¼ yd

 Second light medium . . ⅛ yd

Make four

Additional Yardage for Quilt

Background . . . . . . 1½ yds

 First star border
        one 8" x 16" piece
        two 3½" wide strips…
           …eight 3½" x 6½" pieces
           …four 3½" squares
  Second border
        four 2" wide strips

  Seminole third border
        seven 2⅝" wide strips

First dark . . . . ½ yd

 Seminole third border
        three and a half 2⅝" wide strips

Second dark . . . . . . 1 yd

 First star border
        one 8" x 16" piece
  Fourth border
        five 4¼" wide strips

Binding . . . . ½ yd

         five 3" wide strips

45" x 45"

Backing . . . . 3 yds

Batting . . . . 48" square

Making the First Star Border

1. Use the background and second dark 8" x 16" pieces to draw a 2 x 4 grid of 4" squares.

2. Sew, following Grid Method, page 6.

3. Square the sixteen pieced squares to 3½".

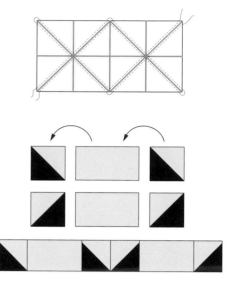

4. Lay out and sew together pieced squares with four background 3½" x 6½" pieces.

   Reverse the order in four additional strips.

5. Sew strips together. Sew two sets to the left and right sides of quilt.

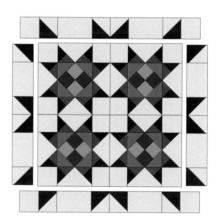

6. Add a 3½" square to each end of the two remaining strips, and sew to top and bottom.

Making the Seminole Border

1. Sew a 2⅝" dark strip between 2⅝" background strips. Press seams to dark side.

2. Cut fifty-six 2⅝" Seminole segments. **Set aside four.**

3. In two stacks of twenty-six lay out staggered segments. Sew pairs.

4. For left and right sides, sew six pairs into a set of twelve and add a single segment.

5. For top and bottom, sew seven pairs into a set of fourteen and add a single segment.

6. Press before cutting.

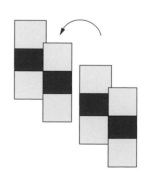

7. Trim long edges, leaving ¼" seam allowance from dark points.

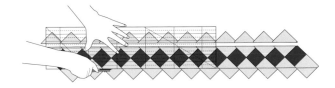

8. Trim ends, leaving ¼" seam allowance beyond dark point.

Finishing the Quilt Top

1. Sew 2" wide background strips to quilt.

2. Press seams toward second border.

3. On each side of the quilt, lay ruler across sewn seams. Draw marks in the seam allowance about every 3" parallel with the star points.

4. On the left and right sides, pin each point of diamond to its mark. With Seminole border on top, sew side borders to quilt, easing or stretching as necessary to fit the length of the background border. Try not to sew through points.

5. Pin and sew top and bottom Seminole borders.

6. **Don't press until fourth border is on.**

Adding the Fourth Border

1. Sew the 4¼" border strips into one long piece.

2. Measure and cut side strips. Pin and sew to quilt.

3. Cut top and bottom strips, pin, and sew to quilt.

Carrie Hall Star

Although Carrie Hall learned to quilt as a child, she didn't pursue it until she began collecting quilt patterns during World War I. She organized her collection into scrapbooks and envelopes, and began stitching a fabric block of each pattern, eventually reaching a total of 850. When the Great Depression threatened her dressmaking business, she began a new career as a lecturer in her mid-sixties. She traveled the state of Kansas with her block collection, speaking to women's study clubs, social clubs, and literary clubs. In 1935 she collaborated with Rose Kretsinger on *The Romance of the Patchwork Quilt in America*, which featured photos of Carrie's quilt blocks.

Cutting Instructions

Layer cut right sides together:

 one 4½" x 9" rectangle background
one 4½" x 9" rectangle first dark

Cut:

 four 2¾" x 4¾" rectangles first dark

 one 4¾" square second dark
or "fussy cut" to appear "on point"

 four 2¾" squares second medium

 four 3½" squares background

Suggested values: *choose the background, two darks, and a medium.*

Making Four of Each

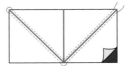

1. Use the 4½" x 9" rectangles right sides together. Draw a 4½" grid of two squares.

2. Sew, cut apart, and press seams to background.

3. Square each patch to 3⅞". Be sure seams end at corners.

4. Cut each on the diagonal, crossing the seam. Do not press bias edges.

Making Four

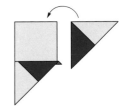

1. In stacks of four, lay out pieced triangles with the corner squares.

2. Flip square to triangle, matching the top and right edges. Assembly-line sew.

3. Clip apart. Fingerpress seam allowance toward triangle.

4. Stack and lay out sewn pieces with remaining pieced triangles.

5. Assembly-line sew triangle to corner square.

6. Press seam allowances to triangles, avoiding bias edge. Trim exposed tips.

Making the Center

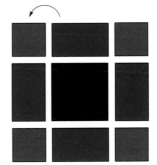

1. Lay out the center, 2¾" squares and rectangles.

2. Sew the vertical seams.

3. Sew the horizontal seams pushing the vertical seam in opposite directions and toward the rectangles.

4. Press horizontal seams toward center.

5. Square to 9".

Sewing the Block Together

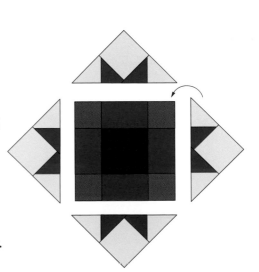

1. Lay out the pieces.

2. Flip and sew opposite corners to center, matching seams. Sew with triangles on top in order to sew across the point. *If piece is too long and needs to be eased in, sew with triangles on bottom.*

3. Press seam allowances toward center.

4. Sew remaining corners. Press seams toward center.

Border Treatment by Patricia Knoechel

Yardage for Four Blocks

Background . . . ½ yd

First dark . . . . ¼ yd

Second dark . . . ¼ yd

Second medium . . ⅛ yd

Make four

Additional Yardage for Quilt

Background . . . . . . 1⅛ yds

Inside lattice
  four 3½" wide strips
Border lattice
  four 4½" wide strips…
    …eight 4½" x block size pieces
    …twelve 4½" x 3½" pieces
    …four 4½" corner squares

First dark . . . . ⅓ yd

Star points
  one 10" wide strip

Second dark . . . . . . ⅛ yd

Star centers
  one 3½" wide strip…
    …nine 3½" squares

Binding . . . . ½ yd

  four 3" wide strips

41" x 41"

Backing . . . . 1¼ yds

Batting . . . . 48" square

Cutting the Lattice

1. Measure the size of your block. Add ⅛" to that measurement to compensate for shrinkage after sewing on star points.

2. Cut twelve lattice (block size plus ⅛") from the 3½" wide strips.

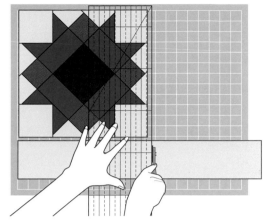

Choosing a Method of Marking Star Point Squares

Choose from these methods to mark and cut squares:

1. Cut 2" strips of star point fabric into (72) 2" squares.

2. Mark diagonal line on the wrong side of each square.

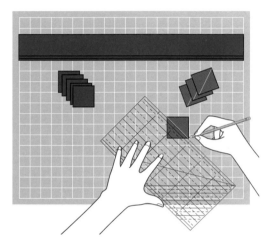

OR

3. Use two 10" x 20" pieces of star point fabric to draw 5 x 10 grids of 2" squares on the back.

4. Draw a diagonal line across each square.

5. Cut into 72 marked squares.

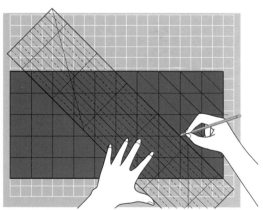

6. Save marking time by using a piece of tape for a diagonal guideline.

Cut a 6" length of ¼" tape. Line up the edge of the tape with the needle. Use the tape as a guide to sew from corner to corner.

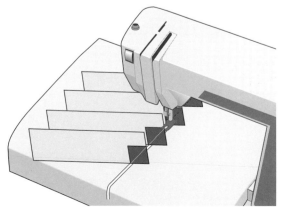

Sewing the Star Point Lattice

1. Place a 2" marked square right sides together to the 3½" lattice, carefully lining up the outside edges.

2. Assembly-line sew **on the diagonal line**, overlapping the top of the new lattice each time.

3. Turn the lattice around and assembly-line sew a second square to each lattice.

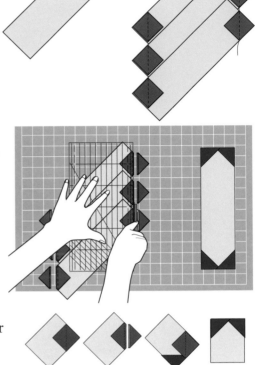

4. Trim seams to ¼" from diagonal line on both sides, and press the star points flat.

5. Assembly-line sew 2" squares to the remaining two corners.

6. Trim seams to ¼" and press the star points flat.

7. Sew 2" squares to one end of the 3½" x 4½" border pieces and trim.

Sewing the Quilt Top Together

1. Lay out the star blocks, the star point lattice and the star centers.

2. Sew the vertical seams.

3. Sew the horizontal seams.

Adding the Star Point Border

1. Sew a star point border piece between 4½" wide border pieces for each side of the quilt.

2. Sew the left and right borders to the quilt.

3. Add a 4½" border corner square to each end of the top and bottom strips.

4. Sew top and bottom borders to the quilt.

Eleanor Roosevelt Star

A buff-colored marble print throws the spotlight on the magnificent chevron border of this variation, in fabrics by Benartex. Kathy chose the same fabric in smoke for her star centers and binding. See instructions on page 77.

Kathy Schaeffer

Eleanor Roosevelt Star

Sue used Flying Geese patches in two fabrics to create an alternating chevron border for her variation, shown here in cool winter shades of blue and burgundy. The folded border forms a striking frame for the floating star blocks. See instructions on page 77.

Sue Bouchard

Frances Willard Star

The attic window lattice of this variation is made with mitered corners, using the same technique as the star centers. Smaller squares in the Flying Geese border repeat the design in lively greens and pinks. See instructions on page 83.

Annitte Hester

In this vibrant layout, Sandy set four stars rotating so that the star points lead the eye toward a striking Seminole border. The wallhanging is free form quilted with invisible thread for an extra finish. See instructions on page 89.

Sandy Thompson

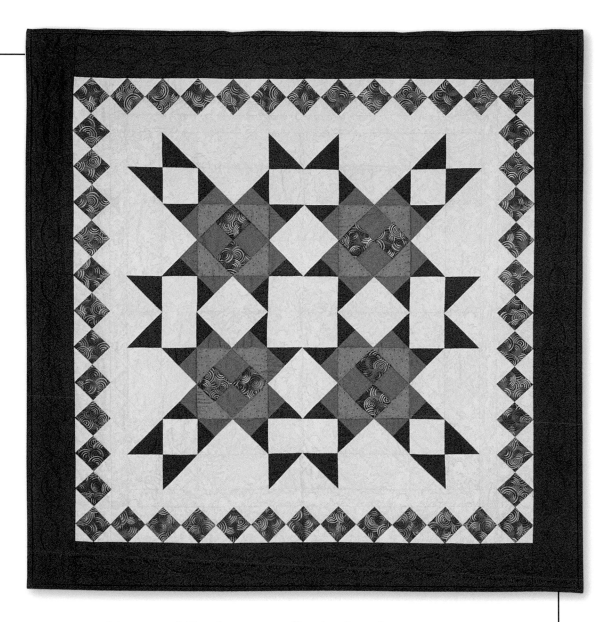

Benartex fabrics in fall colors are well suited to the strong geometrics of this variation. The Seminole border sparkles with a gold embellished print, picking up tones of rust and navy in the stars. Expert machine-quilting adds fine detail to this beautiful wallhanging. See instructions on page 89.

Donna Carter

Fussy cuts steal the show, allowing a charming floral fabric to shine. A star point lattice is a graceful compliment to four star blocks, which feature a richly textured Damask fabric from Benartex in jade green. See instructions on page 94.

Patricia Knoechel

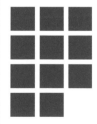

Sheila used Benartex fabrics in purple, mulberry, and gold to give her wallhanging a striking appearance. The same print in white forms a perfect setting for her richly-colored star blocks. See instructions on page 94.

Sheila Meehan

Barbara Frietchie Star

Star blocks of blue and red are accented by smaller stars assembled from triangles. Hearts and flowers, quilted in red, enliven the background of this special setting, also used for the cover quilt. See instructions for Four Point star setting on page 105.

Donna Carter

Settings

Selecting a Setting for Twelve Blocks

The Lattice and Cornerstone setting is the easiest setting for sewing the blocks together into a quilt top. See Loretta Smith's four block wallhanging on page 39. It's quite simple, needing thirty-one 3½" wide x block size pieces, plus twenty 3½" cornerstones. For more of a sewing challenge, select one of the three setting choices on the next seven pages.

Four Point Star Setting by Donna Carter

Yardage for Twelve Block Quilt

Background . . . . . 2¼ yds

Inside lattice
    eleven 3½" wide strips
Border lattice
    seven 4½" wide strips…
        …fourteen 4½" x 15⅝" pieces
        …four 4½" x 7½" pieces

First dark . . . . . 1⅛ yds

Star points
    seven 3½" wide strips…
        …eighty 3½" squares

Second dark . . . . . ½ yd

Star centers
    two 3½" wide strips…
        …twenty 3½" squares

Cutting the Inside Lattice

1. Measure the size of your block. Add ⅛" to that measurement to compensate for shrinkage after sewing on star points.

2. Cut thirty-one lattice (block size plus ⅛") from the 3½" strips, or approximately 12⅝".

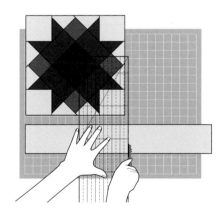

Sewing Two Point Inside Lattice

1. Mark a diagonal line on the wrong side of each square.

Save marking time by using a piece of tape for a diagonal guideline. See page 95.

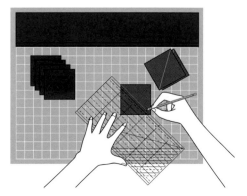

2. Place a 3½" square right sides together to the lattice, carefully lining up the outside edges.

3. Assembly-line **sew on the diagonal lines**, overlapping the top of the new lattice each time.

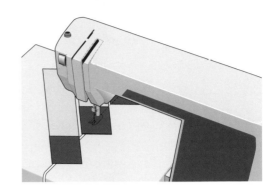

4. Turn the lattice around and assembly-line sew a second square to each lattice.

5. Trim seams to ¼" from diagonal line on both sides, and press the star points flat.

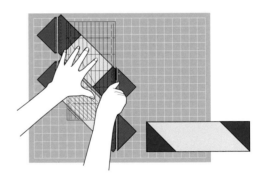

Sewing the Quilt Top Together

1. Lay out the star blocks, star centers, and two point lattice.

2. Sew vertical rows. Pin match star points of lattice to opposite points on block.

3. Sew horizontal rows. Push seams away from star points and toward star centers.

Sewing the One Point Border Lattice

1. Measure your block, and add 3" to that measurement.

2. Cut fourteen pieces approximately 15½" long from the 4½" strips.

3. Place a 3½" square right sides together to the lattice. Assembly-line sew on diagonal line. Trim seams to ¼" from diagonal line, open, and press flat.

4. Sew 3½" squares to one end of the 4½" x 7½" border pieces.

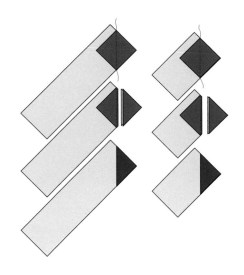

Sewing Border Strips Together

1. Assembly-line sew two rows of three each and two rows of four each.

2. Sew a 4½" x 7½" piece on the left end of each row.

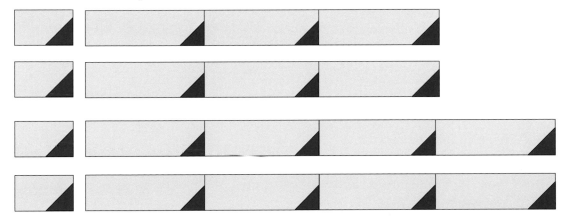

3. Match and pin short border to top of quilt. Leave first 10" unsewn.

4. Pin and sew long border to right side.

5. Pin and sew short border to bottom.

6. Pin and sew long border to left side.

7. Pin and sew remaining 10" on first border.

Eight Point Star Setting for Twelve Blocks

Yardage for Twelve Block Quilt

Background . . . . . . .2¼ yds

Inside lattice
  eleven 3½" wide strips

Border lattice
  seven 4½" wide strips…
    …fourteen 4½" x block size pieces
    …eighteen 3½" x 4½" pieces
    …four 4½" squares

First dark . . . . . . .1⅛ yds

Star points
  two 10" x 20" pieces
  one 10" x 24" piece

Second dark . . . . . . .½ yd

Star centers
  two 3½" wide strips…
    …twenty 3½" squares

Cutting the Lattice

1. Measure the size of your block. Add ⅛" to that measurement to compensate for shrinkage after sewing on star points.

2. Cut thirty-one lattice (block size plus ⅛") from the 3½" wide strips.

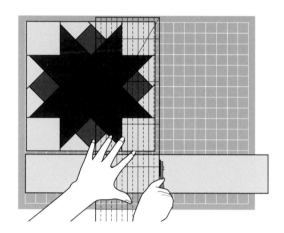

Marking Star Point Squares

1. Draw 5 x 10 grids of 2" squares on the back of two 10" x 20" pieces. Draw a 5 x 12 grid of 2" squares on the back of one 10" x 24" piece.

2. Draw a diagonal line across each square.

3. Cut into 160 marked squares.

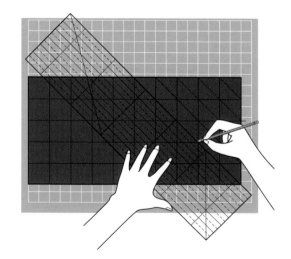

Sewing the Star Point Lattice

1. Place a 2" square right sides together to the 3½" wide lattice, carefully lining up the outside edges.

2. Assembly-line sew **on the diagonal line**, overlapping the top of the new lattice each time.

3. Turn the lattice around and assembly-line sew a second square to each lattice.

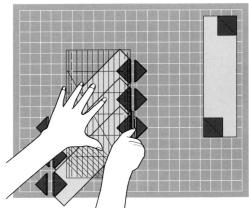

4. Trim seams to ¼" from diagonal line on both sides, and press the star points open and flat.

5. Assembly-line sew 2" squares to the remaining two corners.

6. Trim seams to ¼" and press the star points open and flat.

7. Sew 2" squares to one end of the 3½" x 4½" border pieces and trim.

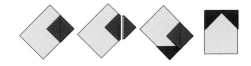

Sewing the Quilt Top Together

1. Lay out the star blocks, the star point lattice, and the star centers.

2. Sew the vertical seams.

3. Sew the horizontal seams.

4. Sew a star point border piece between 4½" wide lattice pieces for each side of the quilt.

5. Sew the left and right borders to the quilt.

6. Add a 4½" square to each end of the top and bottom strips.

7. Sew top and bottom borders to the quilt.

Kaleidoscope Setting for Twelve Blocks by Loretta Smith

Yardage for Twelve Block Quilt

Background . . . . . . .2¼ yds

Lattice
   eleven 6" wide strips…
    …thirty-one 6" x 14½" pieces

If your background fabric is 44" - 45" in width, cut 6" wide strips selvage to selvage to get three 6" x 14½" pieces from each 44" strip.

If your background fabric is less than 44" - 45", cut 6" wide strips lengthwise to get five 6" x 14½" pieces from each 81" strip.

First dark . . . . . . .1⅛ yds

Star points
  five 7¼" wide strips

Second dark . . . . . . .½ yd

Star centers
  three 5½" wide strips…
   …twenty 5½" squares

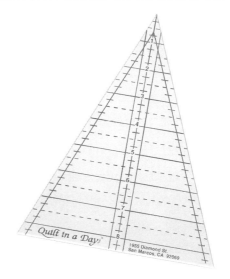

You need a Kaleidoscope ruler (45° angle) to cut triangles for this setting.

Cutting the Triangle Shapes

1. Layer the 7¼" star point strips right sides up on the cutting mat.

2. Line up the 7¼" base line on the Kaleidoscope ruler with the left edge of the fabric.

3. Cut up the right side of the ruler and down, trimming the selvage edge. Remove the excess.

4. Lift and turn the ruler, placing the ruler's 7¼" line across the top edge of the fabric, and the ruler's left edge against the previous cut.

5. Cut again, keeping the lines on the ruler parallel with lines on the grid, until you have a total of 62 triangle shapes.

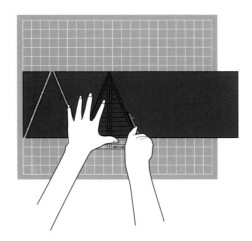

Cutting the Lattice

1. Layer the 6" x 14½" background pieces, and cut on both diagonals.

2. Eliminate two triangles. *These triangles can be used later in a Kaleidoscope quilt.*

3. Stack the long pieces in one stack of 62.

Making the Kaleidoscope Lattice Pieces

1. Place the 62 triangles and 62 background pieces right side up.

2. Flip the triangle onto the lattice. The tip on triangle should **extend ⅜"**. Seam must cross where two pieces meet.

3. Sew, open and check. Seams should create a straight line on long edge. Assembly-line sew all pieces.

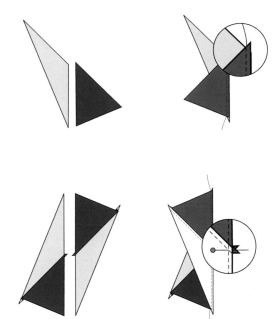

4. Lay sewn piece on ironing board with triangle on top. Set the seam. Lift and press the seam behind the triangle.

5. Stack thirty-one sewn pieces in two piles. Flip the pieces together, positioning them with tips extended to start and stop where they meet in a ¼" seam. **Match and pin the centers.** Assembly-line sew.

7. Press in either direction. Trim center tips.

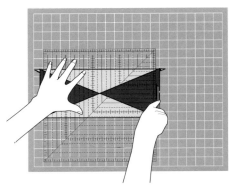

8. Trim lattice to 12½" by centering the 6¼" line on your ruler. Cut away both ends. **This seam does not go into the corner with this angle, unlike patches with 45° angles.** Once the top is sewn together, points will match.

Sewing the Top Together

1. Lay out the blocks with Kaleidoscope lattice and star centers.

2. Flip the second row onto the first. Stack from the bottom to the top so top of row is at top of stack.

3. Assembly-line sew the vertical rows. Do not clip the threads.

4. Sew the horizontal rows, pushing the seams in opposite directions away from the Kaleidoscope lattice and toward the star centers.

Finishing

Creativity in Border Sizes

Suggested border yardage and border examples are given. However, you may wish to custom design the borders by changing the widths of the strips.

When custom fitting the quilt, lay the top on your bed before adding the borders. Measure to find how much border is needed to get the fit you want. Keep in mind that the quilt will shrink approximately 3" in the length and width after machine quilting.

Piecing Borders and Binding Strips

1. Stack and square off the ends of each strip, trimming away the selvage edges.

2. Seam the strips of each fabric into long pieces by assembly-line sewing. Lay the first strip right side up. Lay the second strip right sides to it. Backstitch, stitch the short ends together, and backstitch again.

3. Take the strip on the top and fold it so the right side is up.

4. Place the third strip right sides to it, backstitch, stitch, and backstitch again.

5. Continue assembly-line sewing all the short ends together into long pieces for each fabric.

6. Clip the threads holding the strips together.

7. Press seams to one side.

Sewing the Borders to the Quilt Top

1. Measure down the center to find the length. Cut two side strips that measurement plus two inches.

2. Right sides together, match and pin the center of the strips to the center of the sides. Pin at ends, allowing an extra inch of border at each end. Pin intermittently. Sew with the quilt on top. "Set and direct the seams," pressing toward the borders.

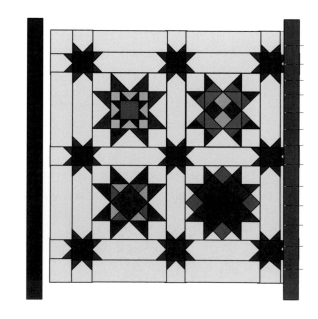

3. Square the ends even with the top and bottom of the quilt.

4. Measure the width across the center including newly added borders. Cut two strips that measurement plus two inches.

5. Right sides together, match and pin the center of the strips to the center of the top and bottom edges of the quilt. Pin at the ends, allowing an extra inch of border at both ends. Pin intermittently. Sew with the quilt on top.

6. "Set and direct the seams," pressing toward the borders. Square the ends even with the side borders. Repeat these steps for additional borders.

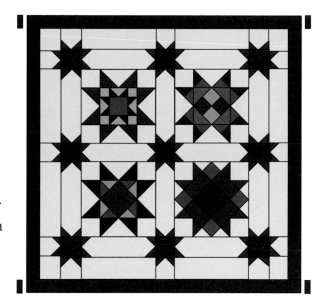

Layering Quilt Top

1. Piece the backing yardage together for larger size quilts.

2. Stretch out the backing right side down on a table or floor. Tape down on a floor area or clamp onto a table with large binder clips.

3. Place and smooth out thin batting on top. Lay the quilt top right side up and centered on top of the batting. Completely smooth and stretch all layers until they are flat. Tape or clip securely.

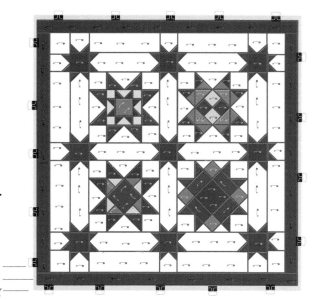

Clamps ———
Batting ———
Backing ———

Quick and Easy Safety Pinning

1. Place safety pins throughout the quilt away from the planned quilting lines. Begin pinning in the center and work to the outside, spacing them every 5".

Grasp the opened pin in your right hand and the pinning tool in your left hand. Push the pin through the three layers, and bring the tip of the pin back out. Catch the tip in the groove of the tool and allow point to extend far enough to push pin closure.

2. Trim backing and batting to 2" on all sides.

Straight Line Quilting

Use this technique for cross-hatch quilting or "stitching in the ditch" around the stars or through the borders.

Machine Set Up

Place a walking foot attachment on your machine. Use invisible thread in the top of your machine and regular thread in the bobbin to match the backing. Loosen the top tension, and lengthen your stitch to 8 - 10 stitches per inch, or a #3 or #4 setting. Free arm machines need the "bed" placed for more surface area.

1. For cross-hatch quilting on background fabric, draw diagonal lines from corner to corner with a silver or soapstone pencil, or piece of chalk.

2. Draw diagonal lines evenly spaced 2" apart from the center diagonal lines in both directions.

3. Use the seam lines as a guide for "stitching in the ditch" around the stars and border.

Quilting with a Walking Foot

1. Roll the quilt tightly from the outside edge in toward middle. Hold this roll with clips or pins.

2. Slide this roll into the keyhole of the sewing machine.

3. Place the needle in the depth of the seam and pull up the bobbin thread. Stitch forward following the design. Pivot with the needle in the fabric. Lock the beginning and ending of each quilting line by backstitching.

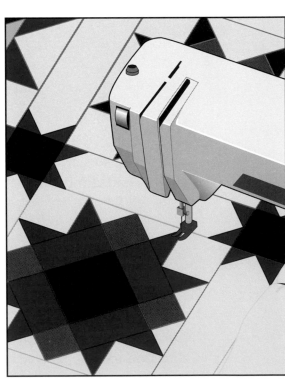

4. Place your hands flat on both sides of the needle to form a hoop. Keep the quilt area flat and tight. If you need to ease in the top fabric, feed the quilt through the machine by pushing the layers of fabric and batting forward underneath the walking foot.

5. Unroll, roll, and machine quilt on all lines, sewing the length or width or diagonal of the quilt.

Free Motion Quilting

Use this technique to outline a stencil design in a background area, fill in background with stippling, or "stitch in the ditch" in the seams of the star blocks. Feed dogs are disengaged, so large, bulky quilts can easily be stitched side to side as well as forward and backward with little manipulation.

Machine Set Up

Use a darning foot or spring needle, and drop the feed dogs or cover with a plate. No stitch length is required as you control the length. Use a fine needle and a little hole throat plate with a center needle position. Use invisible or regular thread in the top and regular thread to match the backing in the bobbin. Loosen the top tension if using invisible thread.

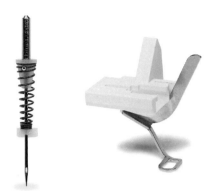

Quilting Around a Stenciled Design or Block

1. Trace a stencil design onto the background fabric.

2. Bring the bobbin thread up on the line of the design or "in the ditch" on a star block. Lower the needle and drop the foot. Moving the fabric very slowly, take a few tiny stitches to lock them. Snip off the tails of the threads.

3. With your eyes watching the outline ahead of the needle, and your fingertips stretching the fabric and acting as a quilting hoop, move the fabric in a steady motion while the machine is running at a constant speed. Keep the top of the quilt in the same position by moving the fabric underneath the needle side to side, and forward and backward. Lock off the tiny stitches and clip threads.

Stippling Your Quilt

Fill in background area with stippling or a meandering stitch.

1. Stitch into the center of the area with a worm-like stitch.

2. Do a curved turn and stitch back in the same direction loosely paralleling the worm-like stitch.

3. Continue to fill in the area with the stippling, being careful not to sew across a line of stitching or across the patchwork.

Adding the Binding

See Piecing Strips, page 112.

Use a walking foot attachment and regular thread on top and in the bobbin to match the binding. Use 10 stitches per inch, or #3 setting.

1. Press the binding strip in half lengthwise with right sides out.

2. Line up the raw edges of the folded binding with the raw edge of the quilt top at the middle of one side.

3. Begin sewing 4" from the end of the binding.

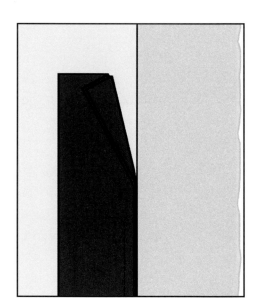

4. At the corner, stop the stitching ¼" from the edge with the needle in the fabric. Raise the presser foot and turn the quilt to the next side. Put the foot back down.

5. Sew backwards ¼" to the edge of the binding, raise the foot, and pull the quilt forward slightly.

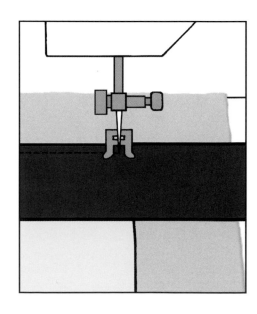

6. Fold the binding strip straight up on the diagonal. Fingerpress in the diagonal fold.

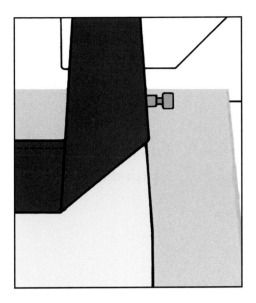

7. Fold the binding strip straight down with the diagonal fold underneath. Line up the top of the fold with the raw edge of the binding underneath.

8. Begin sewing from the corner.

9. Continue sewing and mitering the corners around the outside of the quilt.

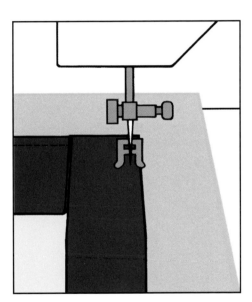

10. Stop sewing 4" from where the ends will overlap.

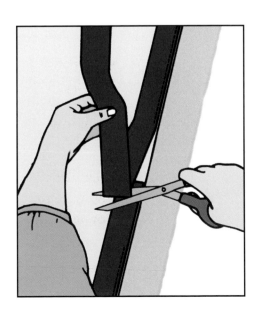

11. Line up the two ends of binding. Trim the excess with a ½" overlap. Open out the folded ends and pin right sides together. Sew a ¼" seam.

12. Continue to sew the binding in place.

13. Trim the batting and backing up to the raw edges of the binding.

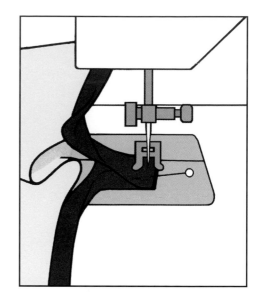

14. Fold the binding to the backside of the quilt. Pin in place so that the folded edge on the binding covers the stitching line. Tuck in the excess fabric at each miter on the diagonal.

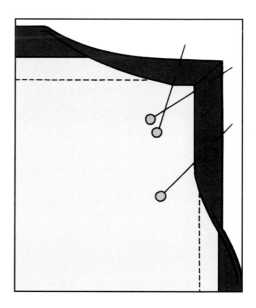

15. From the right side, "stitch in the ditch" using invisible thread on the right side, and a bobbin thread to match the binding on the back side. Catch the folded edge of the binding on the back side with the stitching.

Optional: *Hand slip stitch.*

16. Sew an identification label on the back listing your name, date, and other pertinent information.

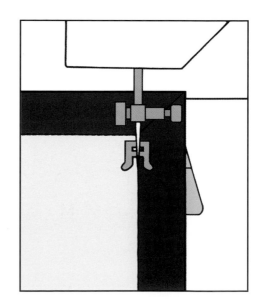

Index

Acknowledgements

A grateful thank you to Benartex for their beautiful fabrics and to my students who tested the instructions.

Special thanks to Loretta Smith, Diane Knight, Linda Dahlman, and Ruth Griffith, for their outstanding work.

My sincere appreciation to the Leavenworth County Historical Museum, the Kansas State Historical Society, and especially Rosalind Webster Perry, for their generous assistance.

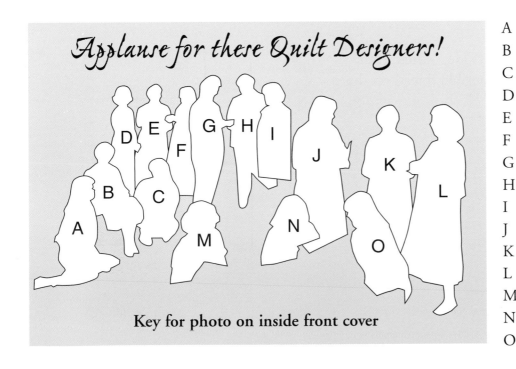

Key for photo on inside front cover

A	Annitte Hester
B	Teresa Varnes
C	Karen Strausheim
D	Sheila Meehan
E	Lois Thornhill
F	Sandy Thompson
G	Donna Carter
H	Pat Wetzel
I	Kathy Schaeffer
J	Eleanor Burns
K	LuAnn Stout
L	Dee Brawley
M	Patricia Knoechel
N	Sue Bouchard
O	Cheryl Minshew

Order Information

Quilt in a Day®, Inc.,
1955 Diamond Street,
San Marcos, CA 92069

Quilt in a Day books offer a wide range of techniques and are directed toward a variety of skill levels. If you do not have a quilt shop in your area, you may write or call for a complete catalog and current price list of all books and patterns published by Quilt in a Day®, Inc.,

Easy

These books are easy enough for beginners of any age.

Quilt in a Day Log Cabin
Irish Chain in a Day
Bits & Pieces Quilt
Trip Around the World Quilt
Heart's Delight Wallhanging
Scrap Quilt, Strips and Spider Webs
Rail Fence Quilt
Dresden Placemats
Flying Geese Quilt
Star for all Seasons Placemats
Winning Hand Quilt
Courthouse Steps Quilt
From Blocks to Quilt

Tulip Quilt
Star Log Cabin Quilt
Burgoyne Surrounded Quilt
Bird's Eye Quilt
Snowball Quilt
Tulip Table Runner

Applique

While these offer a variety of techniques, easy applique is featured in each.

Applique in a Day
Dresden Plate Quilt
Sunbonnet Sue Visits Quilt in a Day
Recycled Treasures
Country Cottages and More
Creating with Color
Spools & Tools Wallhanging
Dutch Windmills Quilt

Holiday

When a favorite holiday is approaching, Quilt in a Day is there to help you plan.

Country Christmas
Bunnies & Blossoms
Patchwork Santa
Last Minute Gifts
Angel of Antiquity
Log Cabin Wreath Wallhanging
Log Cabin Christmas Tree Wallhanging
Country Flag
Lover's Knot Placemats

Sampler

Always and forever popular are books with a variety of patterns.

The Sampler
Block Party Series 1, Quilter's Year
Block Party Series 2, Baskets & Flowers
Block Party Series 3, Quilters Almanac
Block Party Series 4, Christmas Traditions
Block Party Series 5, Pioneer Sampler

Intermediate to Advanced

With a little Quilt in a Day experience, these books offer a rewarding project.

Trio of Treasured Quilts
Lover's Knot Quilt
Amish Quilt
May Basket Quilt
Morning Star Quilt
Friendship Quilt
Kaleidoscope Quilt

Angle Piecing

Quilt in a Day "template free" methods make angle cutting less of a challenge.

Diamond Log Cabin Tablecloth or Treeskirt
Pineapple Quilt
Blazing Star Tablecloth
Schoolhouse Quilt
Radiant Star Quilt

Toll Free: 1 800 777-4852   •   Fax: (619) 591-4424   •   Internet: http://www.quilt-in-a-day.com/qiad/
To order between the hours of 8 am - 5 pm Pacific Time